The Personal Sanity Index

A simple goal-tracking tool
for people who aren't perfect.

Discover the three questions that will
reveal the best version of you!

By Stewart Thornhill, Ph.D.

For Signe, Sarah, and Scarlett

TABLE OF CONTENTS

Introduction

Learn The Best-Kept Secret In
Achieving And Maintaining Highly-Desired Goals And Dreams

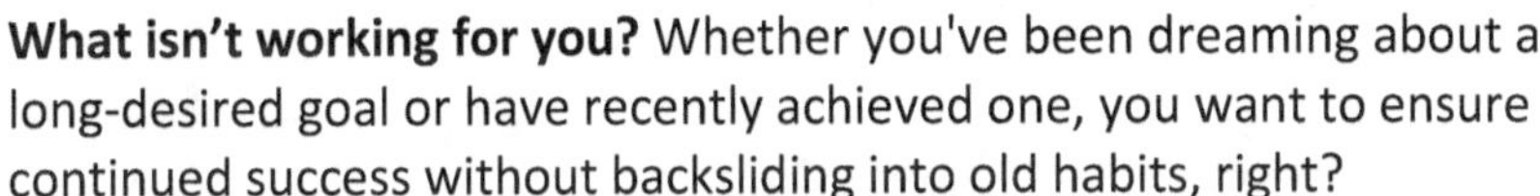

What isn't working for you? Whether you've been dreaming about a long-desired goal or have recently achieved one, you want to ensure continued success without backsliding into old habits, right?

The Personal Sanity Index (PSI) is a simple system designed for people who aren't perfect, helping you reach goals such as living healthier, building better relationships, and finding professional success. And it's not just about getting there—the PSI will help you maintain your achievements over a lifetime.

How? This book starts by uncovering the **three questions** that will reveal the best version of you. Then you will learn how to **lean on this Index**— as your accountability system—to track desired results. With daily use, it will alert you to the danger of veering off course *before it happens*, helping you create a ripple effect of success. That's why it's the only system of its kind.

Do you want to reach for the stars? This system works. With focus and effort, it can help you develop and maintain a healthy lifestyle. By creating a personalized plan that is *best for you* and not the latest fad, you can keep track of daily habits and modify behavior as needed.

It's your life. Discover an outstanding tool for creating and maintaining the best version of you.

Section One

What Is The Personal Sanity Index (PSI)?

"We are what we repeatedly do.
Excellence, then, is not an act, but a habit."
— Aristotle

Chapter 1

What Isn't Working For You?

Is there something you've wanted to achieve for quite some time? Or, maybe you've already made some changes and you don't want to backslide and end up back where you started?

Either way, attaining any goal is only half the battle. Maintaining your new self and continuing to make progress is where the magic happens. (After all, no one wants to push the same boulder up the hill over and over again.)

Consequences

In the quest to continue or become a preferred version of "our future selves," some of us know we need to start a new behavior or stop an old one to achieve optimal results.

Maybe you're one of these people. For example, have you decided you need to lose weight? Or give up an unhealthy habit? Perhaps you want to write a novel or start your own business. Maybe you simply want to wake up every day feeling good instead of feeling exhausted. Or perhaps you've already attained your goal, but you're looking for a proven system to help you maintain your desired results while continuing to gain momentum.

After all, once these milestones are achieved, we need to sustain the improvements, and some consider staying on track the hardest part of the process—whether they're keeping the weight off, getting into the pool each day, saving for retirement, or managing a healthy recovery process.

If we can't maintain our new, preferred way of life, our world consists of the dreaded rollercoaster ride that so many dieters, drinkers, smokers, gamblers, and others have lived with—or want to avoid.

The consequences of not being able to achieve or maintain success can snowball into feelings of failure and hopelessness. Do you feel like you're stuck in a situation where there's no way out? Or are you afraid of backsliding?

Achieving and maintaining success is the foundation of The Personal Sanity Index (PSI). It's a daily accountability system that helps you keep track of how you're doing and makes it possible to catch yourself before you veer off course.

Wouldn't you like a reliable system to help you discover the next step in becoming the best version of you?

Where Do You Start?

This system is based on the idea that striving for constant perfection is unrealistic and unsustainable. Expectations of perfection set people up for failure. The PSI is a simple monitoring system that charts the daily behaviors that are important to you.

It's a simple goal-tracking tool for people who aren't perfect.

It starts with a one-minute daily routine and a customized chart (more on that later) placed in an area you frequent during the day, perhaps in the kitchen when you grab your first cup of coffee. For me, it's the journal I keep on my nightstand. For others, it may be their bathroom mirror or a bulletin board in their home office. There's also a free app you can download and use on your phone.

Could It Be That Simple?

Yes. With daily, consistent tracking, you will have the benefit of using a proven system with decades of research behind it. The science behind the system is drawn from business and engineering, but you don't have to know the math to take advantage of the method. The principles have been adapted to help us manage our daily lives in a simple, stress-free way.

This system has been the foundation in helping me to be my best physically, emotionally, and mentally. As a result, I've maintained my sobriety for three decades, competed in triathlons, and transitioned from a career in engineering to my current role as a professor of entrepreneurial studies. I've also recently achieved a long-held goal of becoming a pilot.

I hope this Index can help you achieve some of your wildest dreams too!

Out Of Sight, Out Of Mind

The adage "out of sight, out of mind" accurately describes a lot of unfinished aspirations, goals, and once-dear hobbies that take up residence in the back of our minds and closets.

We're all guilty of unfinished business.

It's easy to avoid or deny things that are out of view. So, if we want to accomplish something or maintain it, we need to make it a priority while keeping it front-and-center to monitor our progress. It may seem like a small, unimportant detail, but it's amazing how strongly we all respond to things that are in our field of view and how easy it is to neglect things that aren't.

Here's the part you will love. No one expects you to be perfect. There's no such thing! There is even a section dedicated to "variances" to discover when you are going off-track—and course-correct—before it becomes a problem.

I've used it daily for 30 years, and it has enabled me to transform my life.

How Does It Work?

You will use a customized daily Index—created by you—using the app and downloads at personalsanityindex.com, a spreadsheet, or even a pen and paper, if you prefer. This Index will be full of items that are central to your mental, physical, and spiritual health. Examples of these items include your sleep, connections with others, and other things that matter when it comes to keeping you healthy, productive, and sane.

This practice will also give you the foundation to move forward with your highest aspirations using something called Personal Preferences, which we will discuss later.

And yes, you can track all of those things at one time with this Index. I will show you how to create the Index in a later chapter.

The Personal Sanity Index
What Isn't Working For You?

Reflections On Chapter 1

To get the most out of your PSI, copy this question page and document your reactions to this chapter's content. Take time to consider the questions, answer honestly, and create a journal using these pages as your writing prompts and inspiration.

1. Is there something you've wanted to achieve for quite some time that you haven't? What is it?

____

____

____

____

2. Have you recently accomplished something, and now you're afraid of backsliding? What is it?

____

____

____

____

3. Do you want to stop an old behavior or start a new one? If so, which behavior(s)?

____

____

____

____

Chapter 2

Why Listen To Me?

So far, I hope you're intrigued by the idea of using this Index because my goal is to help as many people as I can. You may be wondering if you even need your own Personal Sanity Index and, if so, why am I the person who can help you uncover a solution for what isn't working for you?

That's fair. So, I'd like to tell you a little about me and my challenges, including how and why I developed this system.

I believe the reason no one else developed and refined this simple system—even though there's research dating back to the 1950s proving its success—is because it's more exciting to attain a goal than stick with it. Fad diets are all about the hype of losing so many pounds in a matter of weeks. But what about after the novelty has faded? Then it's just you and the bathroom scale on your own again.

The gym you joined doesn't care about the longevity of your goal. Once you've bought into a diet or exercise program, they have your money, and they move on to the next prospect. Even if you manage to achieve your short-term goals, they're off selling their program to a new customer while hoping you're on autopilot.

What if, instead, someone was interested in helping us preserve our gains and maintain our successes? This book was developed to help you do just that.

In my career as a manufacturing quality engineer, I realized that successful companies are only as good as the products they make. That means hour after hour, year after year, consistent quality is the goal, and we can use those same principles of measurement and monitoring to preserve our own hard-won accomplishments. That's the premise of the PSI system, proven to work based on a personalized plan that is designed by you and for you. By keeping track of daily habits and modifying your behavior as needed, this becomes an essential tool for living healthier, building better relationships, and finding professional success.

Why did I create it? I did it to save my life. At the age 26, I was so out of control that I ended up in a hospital's detox ward, fighting for my life.

On The Brink Of Bankruptcy And Death

My story involves addiction and recovery. That doesn't mean you have to be in recovery or have experienced trauma or other significant challenges for the system to work for you. That just happened to be the path I followed and, because of it, I was able to connect the dots between my personal life and the tools and techniques I used every day in the workplace.

My problems with alcohol started in the seventies, at the age of 13, when my parents' liquor cabinet was fully stocked and unsupervised. In that era, and in the small town where I grew up, being able to hold your liquor was a sign of status. In my case, it was how I defined manhood.

Over the years, I continued to raise the bar on my levels of consumption, far outpacing the typical frat boy or barfly. Looking back, it's hard to fathom the quantities of alcohol that I consumed daily in search of a buzz. Eventually, I stopped seeking pleasure and just wanted to feel numb. The world was simpler that way, and I didn't have to deal with the emotional challenges of daily life.

By the time I was 26, things were so bad that I was living in a constant state of depression and on the brink of bankruptcy with my job crushing down on me. Because of my addiction, I was teetering on the edge of certain death. Blackouts were normal. The spiral of addiction and despair was getting deeper and spinning faster.

My girlfriend of many years kicked me out when she realized that drinking was more important to me than she was. My daily goal was to nurse the hangover I woke up with so I could go back to the liquor store after work, buy more of the precious liquid, and start the process all over again.

Lather. Rinse. Repeat.

It turned out that being rejected—from my relationship and my home—was the kick in the butt I needed. We saw a couple's counselor, but rather than discuss the relationship, the counselor immediately focused on my alcohol consumption. She said, in no uncertain terms, that we'd never be able to save our relationship if I didn't stop drinking.

At first, it was shocking to me: Is she accusing me of being an alcoholic? And how many of our relationship issues were due to what I've considered to be a "bad habit?"

Yet, I knew one thing was true: I loved the oblivion of drinking.

Suddenly, the other "excuses" for the failure of our broken future were drowned out by the excess of my uncontrollable addiction. I looked in the mirror and was horrified by what I saw.

I'd lost a lot of weight because food had stopped tasting good. In fact, I often found myself choking down a can of tuna while standing at the kitchen sink to consume enough calories to be a functional human being at work each day.

After all, the bulk of my weekly paycheck was budgeted for booze, not food.

The dark circles under my eyes told the story. The constant, pungent smell emanating from my pores was undeniable. Beer, wine, vodka, it didn't matter. It all came to the surface eventually, just like my constant state of denial.

What Was I Thinking?

I wondered if the people I worked with in the engineering department or on the plant floor knew about my secret, which only felt like a bad habit at the time. There were three guys that I carpooled with to the factory every day. I noticed how the energy shifted whenever I entered the car.

Was I being paranoid, or did they know my secret? As depressed as I was about how out of control my life had become, I was also terrified that people would discover how much of a loser I really was. Fear and shame made it hard to reach out, hard to connect with people, and especially hard to ask for help.

One day, during lunch in the cafeteria, I realized that I had to stop ordering soup because my hands shook so severely from daily alcohol withdrawal. By the time the utensil made it to my mouth, there wasn't any chicken noodle left on the spoon. But, like a true addict, my immediate reaction was to change from soup to a sandwich rather than do anything about the cause of my trembling hands.

The Personal Sanity Index
Why Listen To Me?

Reflections on Chapter 2

To get the most out of your PSI, copy this question page and document your reactions to this chapter's content. Take time to consider the questions, answer honestly, and create a journal using these pages as your writing prompts and inspiration.

1. Is there a failure from the past that is haunting you? Is fear holding you back from taking a next step? Describe it in detail.

2. Do you feel like you're stuck in a situation with no way out? Describe it in detail.

Chapter 3

How Did I Turn Things Around?

Listening to the therapist was a wake-up call for me. I wanted to work things out with my girlfriend, and I knew I couldn't do that in my condition. I had to acknowledge defeat and ask for help.

It was tough for a lone, do-it-yourselfer. Asking for help ran against every instinct I had. I grew up believing that men are self-sufficient and should be able to handle anything.

But, I knew that if I didn't get sober in my twenties, I wouldn't make it to my thirties. I was playing Russian Roulette with drunk driving, the possibility of burning the house down with a cigarette after passing out, or a list of other possibilities that haunted me.

On May 6th, 1991, at the age of 26, I checked myself into a hospital to dry out. When they took a breath sample, my blood-alcohol was double the legal limit—and it was the morning after!

After four days of sleep (up to 20 hours a day) and IVs to ease the alcohol withdrawal, my body began to recover. Exhausted from the abuse I'd done to myself, a restorative sleep took over. But the physical detox was only the beginning.

What's Next?

I left the hospital, hoping to find a recovery program. AA gave me a dependable roadmap and proven instructions that included 12 steps. I read them and started taking action without deviating from their 30-meetings-in-30-days plan. This strategy helps to instill a new behavior until it becomes a habit.

AA doesn't work for everyone, but it worked for me. I was also lucky to get a spot in a 28-day rehab program less than a month later. Together, they saved my life by giving me tools I needed to cope.

But, I was desperate to find a way to stay sober after wasting ten years of my life in a state of numbness, isolation, denial, and deception.

One Day At A Time

Rehab was an intense month with great counselors who listened. I often heard myself talking about issues that I didn't know were affecting me. Anyone who's undergone counseling or therapy may discover that it's not the things we know about that are our greatest challenges, but often it's the traumas and events that are buried deep in our subconscious memories. Out of sight, out of mind.

For example, I carried the heartache of the death of my infant brother into my adult years without even realizing it. After therapy, I learned that this early trauma was among the reasons I sought to numb myself.

Being surrounded by non-judgmental people who understood my challenges was a great way of receiving some much-needed validation. Ultimately, they wanted me to get excited about my life and think about building a new future for myself.

But one of my core issues became exceedingly obvious: I had no idea how to interact with humans when sober. Just getting through a day was tough, but *forever?*

It was apparent that I would need to learn essential coping skills.

I felt like I was starting over with all kinds of things, like eating a healthy diet and incorporating moderate exercise. I was still smoking, which made any physical activity more difficult. That's when the "one day at a time" philosophy started speaking to me. Imagining decades of sobriety stretched out in front of me—which is where I am now—seemed an impossible feat at the time.

Next Steps

I remember having a lot of special moments during my treatment at Crosbie House in Nova Scotia, and one, in particular, stands out. The program was run by two recovery counselors—both more than 20 years sober—in a house in the country. About 30–40 people rotated through the four weeks of the curriculum at any given time.

One day, George, the head counselor, held a group session and said, "Listening to you, Stewart, I think you'd be a great teacher. Have you thought about getting your Ph.D.?"

At that point, I'd thought about getting my MBA (mostly to find something to do that wasn't in a factory setting) and I'd even taken the exams before going into rehab. In fact, I went to a bar the night before the exams and was hungover the day of testing. But that was normal for me as a functioning alcoholic.

Fortunately, I got a good score on the exam and started receiving applications for graduate programs at top schools like Harvard and Stanford. At the time, I couldn't imagine filling them out because it was like getting applications from Mars.

It felt like a joke to me. I threw the applications out. I remember thinking, *obviously, they don't know what they're doing.* No one in my small town had ever gone to a prestigious university. Because I didn't have a role model, I didn't even consider it.

It seemed absurd to me.

Don't Mistake The Edge Of The Rut For The Horizon

At first, I couldn't imagine a future that included getting my doctorate. But for the first time in a long time, I started visualizing new possibilities and getting excited about the future. I realized I needed to find (or build) a solid strategy to be resilient over the disease during fragile times. I needed something with a series of checks and balances to keep me grounded. Centered. Sane.

What I hadn't realized was that I was already building my strategy by doodling in my journal every day with the beginnings of my first Index.

A New Normal

Another special memory I have from the recovery program includes the time I was tossing a frisbee with new friends and I found myself laughing—without being intoxicated—for the first time in years.

I felt joy in simple ways by allowing connections to happen, even though this was one of the things that scared me the most about going out into the world sober. I started feeling hopeful about doing normal things like going to the movies, restaurants, etc., without the need for liquid courage.

Important Lessons

One reason I was hesitant to consider that I had a drinking problem was because there was so much of it around me growing up.

It seemed *normal.*

Later, I came to understand that some people have a predisposition to addictive behavior based on their genetics. As it turns out, I'm on the 50/50 nature-nurture spectrum. I have a family history of alcoholism that no one had discussed with me.

In recovery, I also discovered that around 10% of the population has a predisposition for addiction and drinking in excess. Starting from an early age also affects one's brain chemistry, stunting one's emotional maturity and freezing development.

Consequently, when I got sober at 26, I had the emotional maturity of a teenager, *and it took me years* to slowly learn how to function as a full-grown adult.

I was lucky because I was able to spend that time in the relatively sheltered world of grad school and, later, teaching in Japan. It was an opportunity to try my hand at academia while considering earning a Ph.D., with the ultimate goal of teaching in a university.

The Personal Sanity Index
How Did I Turn Things Around?

Reflections on Chapter 3
To get the most out of your PSI, copy this question page and document your reactions to this chapter's content. Take time to consider the questions, answer honestly, and create a journal using these pages as your writing prompts and inspiration.

1. Do you feel like you need a wake-up call? Is something or someone around you taking too much of your time and attention? What needs to change?

____

____

____

____

____

____

2. Is there a non-judgmental person in your life with whom you can share your goals and dreams for the future?

____

____

____

____

____

Chapter 4

With A Little Help From My Friends

After 28 days in rehab, I had a heavy heart as I headed out into the real world. This was a worrisome time for me, even though I was healthier than I'd been after a decade of unrelenting addictions.

I was back in the working world while trying to interact with people, yet I was obsessed with new problems that came as a result of my newly minted sobriety.

Topping the list was the need to stay on track and not backslide into alcohol dependency. *That weighed heavily on my mind.* I didn't know it then, but the Index would help me keep my sobriety, soon becoming my faithful companion.

Next, since I had been using alcohol to sedate myself for years, I constantly worried about sleep because I'd adopted a strategy for the past decade that involved drinking until I passed out. The question was, would I be able to get a good night's rest without it? It turned out my fear was unfounded. Once my body rebalanced, sleep became a welcome friend.

Finally, the prospect of facing my carpool buddies terrified me when I was in rehab. I spent a lot of time playing over the nasty (but justified) things they would say about me regarding my absence and stupidity in getting myself into such a no-win situation.

That one paralyzed me. I was expecting they would see me as weak and useless, and I was overwhelmed with shame at the prospect.

It's Time To Take My Punishment

On my first day back to work, true to form, my three carpool friends stopped in my driveway to pick me up.

I cringed as I got into the car and waited. When you've been hiding a drinking problem for a long time, it's important no one knows. After all the deception, I knew my secret was out.

The volume of shame was terrifying.

It was time to take my punishment.

But Mike simply said, "Wow! You look better." And then they talked about what happened in the hockey playoffs the night before.

That was it.

They didn't bust my chops. They didn't tease me endlessly, and all the stress I had caused myself during rehab was *baseless.*

After a month of intense therapy, I couldn't help but wonder why I did that to myself. How often did I visualize negative outcomes—based on a need for deep-seated perfectionism—that stopped me from making positive steps forward?

As I pondered this, I considered continuing therapy outside of rehab, wondering what else might be holding me back.

In the end, I realized my friends were just happy to see me breathing and upright and were collectively worried about my state of depression and dangerous addictions. That day they each confessed that they knew I wasn't long for this world at the rate I was going. It was a sad thing to hear.

Once I realized that they cared about me, I was able to relax. And I appreciated our friendship.

The Personal Sanity Index
With A Little Help From My Friends

Reflections on Chapter 4

To get the most out of your PSI, copy this question page and document your reactions to this chapter's content. Take time to consider the questions, answer honestly, and create a journal using these pages as your writing prompts and inspiration.

1. Do you have a secret that's crushing you? Can you find someone (a friend or counselor) with whom you can talk about it?

____

____

____

____

2. Have you ever imagined negative consequences that you later found baseless, causing you unnecessary grief? If so, what were they?

____

____

____

____

3. Has fear kept you from accomplishing something potentially extraordinary?

____

____

____

____

Chapter 5

If You're Not Perfect, This System Is For You!

I was finally starting to feel good about life again. But something was haunting me. As I replayed some of my counseling sessions in my mind, I realized I had *unfulfilled* goals. I didn't like working in the tire factory, but I was terrified because I had no other life skills.

Shame and fear were abundant in those days, but as I hurdled over challenges—large and small—I started feeling a newfound confidence.

So, two months into my newfound sobriety, I quit my job in the tire factory and moved to Vancouver to earn my MBA at the University of British Columbia.

My girlfriend came with me. We relied on each other a lot because we didn't know anyone. As the breadwinner, she worked at a hotel while I went to school. Someday, I hoped I'd be able to return the favor.

After I moved, I also quit smoking. I had been a card-carrying member of the "pack-a-day" club for eight years.

Looking back, it occurs to me that experts tell us not to take on too many significant life stressors—within a single year—for a good reason. Yet, I foolishly checked off several within the first six months of my fragile sobriety: I gave up alcohol and smoking, quit my job, moved across the country, reestablished my relationship, and began studying at a new school to earn my MBA.

It wasn't a good idea, but, despite my questionable choices, I managed to stay sober. I had a system. And it worked.

How Did I Do It All?

I attribute my success across the board to using the Personal Sanity Index, which, in its infancy in 1991, consisted of rudimentary daily journal entries. I didn't understand it at the time, but I was using a modified component of Quality Assurance adopted from the techniques I'd used and taught to others during my career as a manufacturing engineer.

Quality Assurance is used in manufacturing to achieve and maintain desired quality levels in products and services. The process works by understanding *what* affects quality, then putting systems in place to keep track of whether each stage of the process is performing the way it should.

It's a simple process that includes four stages: Plan, Do, Check, and Act (PDCA), which monitors progress.

For more than half a century, Quality Assurance was—and continues to be—the gold standard in achieving *desired* outcomes. Chances are, this principle has touched many things you enjoy in your daily life (such as electronics, home goods, etc.) because companies worldwide use this system.

By turning my journal into a personal index that tracked daily behaviors with the end result clearly in focus, I soon realized that by paying stricter attention to *each stage* in the process (of training to compete in a triathalon, for example), I could more successfully achieve my goals.

I knew Quality Assurance had decades of research behind it, so it stood the test of time. Companies, industries, and entire countries had bet their success on it and, over the years, I watched it pay off time and time again.

I knew it worked!

One of my favorite stories about Quality Assurance took place in the 1950s. The US wanted to have better relations with the Japanese after the war, so we sent an American consultant to teach them about the process, and they took it seriously.

As a result, Japanese automakers became number one in the world for quality!

Just Enough To Be Dangerous

Luckily, my knowledge of Quality Assurance included the *nuances* of knowing when it did and *didn't* work. I created a similar system for my personal use (mainly for keeping my sobriety under control) while having the ability to stack the deck in my favor.

I compared the factory set-up to the human condition while monitoring several vital areas at once in my quest to live a better life. It occurred to me that I might combine different aspects of well-being into a simple, easy-to-use tool.

If so, what would it look like and how would it work?

Better yet, would other people be interested in such a system?

Do You Want To Flourish and Thrive?

Over time, I moved from journal entries to a spreadsheet and created columns to help me work on my goals daily while monitoring them weekly and monthly.

Even though real-life circumstances aren't as predictable as the assembly lines in a manufacturing plant, several things intrigued me about using the Quality Assurance process for desired personal outcomes. It always started by asking three simple questions:

1. What isn't working?
2. What would I rather have?
3. What needs to happen (repeatedly) to succeed?

All of these questions will be addressed for you later in the book, when your Personal Sanity Index begins to take shape!

Keeping Goals Front And Center

In the factory setting, I also noted that the engineers documented the measurements on a chart positioned directly in front of the factory operator. It wasn't in a drawer or a three-ring binder to be overlooked. It was on a clipboard right in his/her line of sight, which kept it as a priority.

We know that any process in the real world has some natural **variance.** As long as the variance is within acceptable limits, the process is "in control." When a measurement is outside the tolerance, it's a signal to shut down, investigate, and get things back to specifications. Control charts also indicate if a trend is developing. If three measurements in a row are trending in an undesirable direction, that alerts the operator that something may be going on so he or she can address it before things get outside of tolerance and cause real problems.

I realized that, even though people aren't machines, we also have natural variance in our daily actions and routines. Some of those things are tolerable, others can send us spiraling out of control. The Personal Sanity Index is simply a control chart for daily life. And it's based on the same three simple questions: *what isn't working, which outcome do I prefer, and what needs to happen (repeatedly) to ensure success?*

Today, there are four primary categories that I track daily to maintain my own mental and physical health. I've found that if I let just one of these slip, it affects other things, including my daily *productivity*—just like the manufacturing plant!

In 1991 and the decades since, my focus became *maintaining* my progress while developing and monitoring new goals to become the best version of myself.

I knew I was onto something as I continued to strive for a life where I could *flourish and thrive!*

Consider this: Your time, energy, and attention are limited. Let the Index track your progress so you feel like you're in control of life instead of the other way around—for the sake of your sanity.

The Personal Sanity Index
If You're Not Perfect, This System Is For You!

Reflections on Chapter 5

To get the most out of your PSI, copy this question page and document your reactions to this chapter's content. Take time to consider the questions, answer honestly, and create a journal using these pages as your writing prompts and inspiration.

1. Have you ever reached a goal but started to backslide when there was a variance?

____

____

____

____

2. Did a variance lead to failure? If so, list your unreached goals here.

____

____

____

____

3. If you could access a simple, customized way to track your own mental and physical health, would you use it?

____

____

____

____

Chapter 6

Is Self-Neglect The Real #1 Cause Of Death In The US?

As a whole, we Americans neglect our physical and mental health in staggering numbers. According to the Centers for Disease Control and Prevention (CDC), **more than 40% of the US population is clinically obese.**[1] **Obesity accounts for 20% of total health care costs.**[2]

Less than 25% of Americans meet daily exercise guidelines,[3] and **lack of sleep costs the economy more than $400 billion each year.**[4] **The economic costs of mental illness are in the trillions worldwide,**[5] while the human costs are incalculable.

Preventable?

Cancer, cardiovascular disease, and diabetes are all affected by adequate amounts of sleep, exercise, and nutrition. Paying attention to our health is not just about helping us look and feel better. For some, it can be a matter of life and death.

What these statistics are telling us is that—as individuals—we are in control of our health, and we either don't realize it or turn a blind eye to it. I hear people blame their poor self-care on their genetics, over-whelming jobs, families, and schedules. Sometimes it takes a trip to the emergency room or some mounting health challenge before they get a clue.

I've been guilty of this too. For me, it took a failing relationship, poor health with daily blackouts, being on the edge of bankruptcy, and living in a constant state of depression before I opened my eyes. I want to help people realize *the power is in our hands!*

The Personal Sanity Index
Is Self-Neglect The Real #1 Cause Of Death In The US?

Reflections on Chapter 6
To get the most out of your PSI, copy this question page and document your reactions to this chapter's content. Take time to consider the questions, answer honestly, and create a journal using these pages as your writing prompts and inspiration.

1. Are there areas of self-neglect in your life? What is the first you'd like to address?

\
\
\
\
\
\

2. Which short-term behaviors will help you turn things around for the better in the long-term?

\
\
\
\
\
\

28

Section Two

Introducing The PSI: How Does It Work?

*"Doing the best at this moment puts you in
the best place for the next moment."*
— Oprah Winfrey

Stewart Thornhill, Ph.D.

Chapter 7

Nourishing The Body, Mind, and Spirit
(Introducing The Core Four)

In this section, I will cover how the Index works and introduce you to the Core Four and your Personal Preference Categories. These will help you discover what you *really* want in life to create the best version of you.

In the next section, you will create your journal while building your Index, but don't skip ahead, because this introductory section is the foundation for building it later.

As mentioned, this scientifically based system will help you achieve or maintain certain goals while using a proven system with decades of research behind it.

Now, let's dig in.

There are *two distinct parts* of the Personal Sanity Index:

1. The Core Four, covered in this chapter, which are the basic necessities in developing and maintaining a healthy foundation for your everyday well-being, and

2. Your Personal Preferences, covered in the next chapter, which will help you accomplish big things!

The Core Four

I've found that everything starts with the Core Four categories because we simply cannot expect ourselves to accomplish other, *loftier goals* if our *basic needs* aren't met.

As top medical experts will attest, "living well" depends on our ability to get enough sleep (seven-plus hours are a necessity), eating nutritious "real" food, exercising regularly, and fulfilling interpersonal connections. These can be assessed in your workbook and tracked on your Index.

The Core Four:
1. Sleep
2. Food
3. Exercise
4. Connection

Even though we all have different specific needs and wildly different goals, these essential criteria will help you in your quest to *live your best life.*

1. SLEEP. (Why Prioritizing Sleep Isn't One Big Snore)
I'm amazed at how many people deprive themselves of sleep, night after night, week after week, for years—even decades. Often, I find people *think* they are getting adequate sleep by going to bed at midnight or later, then they curse their 6 o'clock alarm every morning.

This isn't a great way to start each day, yet, some people think it's normal and are unapologetic about it like it's a badge of honor as they brag, "I get by on five or six hours of sleep a night."

Get. By.

They blame their self-imposed sleep schedules on time constraints and will tell you they're certain there isn't an alternative. They chronically complain about being tired, and it's a drain on their health, their careers, and their relationships (because people are *tired* of hearing about it).

According to the Centers for Disease Control and Prevention: ***"Adults need 7 or more hours of sleep per night for the best health and well-being. Short sleep duration is defined as less than 7 hours of sleep per 24-hour period."***[6]

A True Story

Years ago, I had a colleague who went to his yearly physical complaining of heart palpitations. As a devout business owner, he put his time and energy into managing his employees, finding the best technology to expand his reach, and attracting new clients.

At the age of 49, David was shocked to learn that he was a candidate for open-heart surgery. The doctor told him the first thing he needed to change was his sleep schedule. "Getting by" on six hours a night wasn't helping him get the right amount of rest to recharge for the next day.

When his doctor talked to him about the Core Four—although he didn't call them that—he told him his lack of sleep was contributing to his weight gain and mental exhaustion. All of that could lead to a heart attack.

David immediately started an exercise program and created a more serious sleep schedule. He even lost 20 pounds over several months and hoped the worst was behind him. But, a year later, he discovered he needed a quadruple bypass.

After years of not getting enough sleep and eating poorly, the damage was done.

The good news is, he's doing fine today, but he might have avoided a life-threatening disease and a life-saving surgery if he'd taken his health seriously in his younger days.

How many of us are creating health issues by neglecting the basics of sleep?

CONSIDER THIS: For a week, track how many hours of quality sleep you get each night on your Core Four Index. If it's below the 7-8 recommended hours, start making sleep a *priority*. Do this by going to bed *earlier*.

Also, make a note of how rested you feel each day so you can figure out how much sleep you need. It's your Index, so it's essential to understand what *your* body needs.

If you have sleep issues, do some research and consider consulting a professional for help. Personally, I've found that a hard cut-off for email and news at 7:00 PM gives me a mental cooling-off period before bedtime. Blue light filters, white noise machines, and other simple tools and techniques can also make a significant difference.

So, the next time you think about curling up with a good book, your dog, or your pillow (which may also be your dog), think about all of the health benefits of sound slumber.

2. FOOD. (Glorious Food)

Our love/hate relationship with food has significant consequences. As discussed earlier, the medical community is telling us that several preventable health issues are making us sick and killing us in record numbers. With obesity documented in significant numbers throughout the US, how and what we eat is too important to ignore.

Here's The Question

Why are we human beings so confused about how we should feed ourselves? Other species on this planet do not have this problem. Decades ago, we complicated things when we created processed foods and labeled them as "nutritious."

Now we have a massive problem with generations of people who simply don't know how they should eat. Getting back to basics, like eating naturally grown food, is a simple answer for everyone.

There are so many dangers to consider! It starts with profiteers peddling addictive junk foods in the overflowing aisles of our grocery stores combined with "health" gurus extolling the virtues of nutrition-limiting fad diets. And too many communities suffer from food deserts, relying on fast food because they don't have access to fresh markets and grocery stores.

Good News: It Doesn't Have To Be Complicated!

Health experts tell us the **foundation** of healthy eating is a diet based on the daily consumption of fruits and vegetables. *Improvising* with processed foods is backfiring, causing a snowball effect over time. It doesn't mean you have to become a vegetarian. But, for most of us, increasing the amount of plants in our diet—especially those with minimal processing—is a good idea.

The Best Strategy In Preventing Obesity And Chronic Diseases

According to the CDC: ***"Eating a diet high in fruits and vegetables is associated with a decreased risk of many chronic diseases, including heart disease, stroke, high blood pressure, diabetes, and some cancers."***[7]

The CDC Guide suggests many options, even for food deserts. For example, they recommend starting your own garden, creating a food council, and expanding farmers' markets in your community.

If you are struggling with healthy eating, contact a professional who can help you create a plan that works for you. Plot it in your journal, then use the Index to track your progress.

CONSIDER THIS: For a week, track your *normal* eating patterns, including what you eat, how much, and how often in your journal/workbook. This will give you a starting point. Most people are shocked at the lack of fruits and veggies in their diet.

I can't tell you how many calories you need or what combination of foods to eat or to avoid, but if you pay attention to what you eat and how you feel afterward, you can probably figure out what you need and what works (and doesn't) for you. The Index won't ask how many calories or grams of protein you consume, but you will want to assess whether a given day was a good one for food consumption or not. It's only you, so be honest.

I have a colleague who has been doing this for the past 12 months. She makes sure she eats 1-2 servings of fruits and veggies with each meal. No counting calories, no complications. She has lost the weight, kept it off, and is now rewarding herself by wearing clothes that had been pushed to the back of the closet for way too long.

3. EXERCISE. (What Kind Of Activities Do You Like?)

Isaac Newton, one of the most influential scientists of all time, was famous for his First Law of Motion, which states: *"An object at rest stays at rest, and an object in motion stays in motion."*

Which one of these defines your active lifestyle?

Walk, Dance, Hike, Bike, Swim

According to the CDC, regular physical activity is one of the *most important things* you can do for your health, and moderate-intensity aerobic activity, such as brisk walking, is generally safe for most people. Their recommendation is 150 minutes each *week.*

The CDC states: ***"We know 150 minutes each week sounds like a lot of time, but it's not. That could be 30 minutes a day, five days a week. The good news is that you can spread your activity out during the week, so you don't have to do it all at once."*** [8]

Moderate intensity means you're working hard enough to raise your heart rate and break a sweat. One way to tell if you've achieved this level of intensity is that you'll be able to *speak,* but not *sing,* the words to a song.

For some, daily movement can be as simple as walking to the store and carrying the bags home or taking long, vigorous walks four days a week. In my case, I've found that if I exercise every day, I'll sustain injuries. Four times a week is optimum for me, keeping me at peak performance.

CONSIDER THIS: Experts cite the key to sticking with an exercise routine is finding something you love—or at least like—to do. Moderate intensity can include walking, hiking, biking, dancing, swimming, or even mowing the lawn. If you try an activity and hate it, that's probably not the right one for you. Just keep looking until you get the right match.

Move more. Sit less.

4. CONNECTION. (Surround Yourself With People You Love And Respect)
Even though I spent many years isolating myself and trying to act as though that was "normal," human beings are social creatures. Our need for interpersonal relations starts early in life. As children, some of our most basic needs involve love, affection, and emotional connection. Sharing loving relationships early in life helps us feel worthy and lovable.

According to research at Stanford University: ***"People who feel more connected to others have lower levels of anxiety and depression. Moreover, studies show they also have higher self-esteem, greater empathy for others, are more trusting and cooperative, and, as a consequence, others are more open to trusting and cooperating with them."***[9]

Strong social connections can also help you live longer!

We Need Each Other

We all need a circle we can count on during the good times and the bad. I'm lucky because I have "running" friends, "work" friends, and a great family—but I also know I've had to work on building these connections over time. It hasn't been natural or easy for me.

CONSIDER THIS: In prioritizing my interpersonal connections as part of my Core Four, I've vastly improved my mental and emotional health, which I'm sure has also positively affected my physical health. Consequently, I have a tribe I can count on to support me through tough times—just as I'm there for them.

According to *Psychology Today*, ***"...studies show our emotional needs are an integral and healthy part of our adult operating system and compel us to create secure attachments. This is important because loneliness can be as detrimental to our health as obesity or smoking 15 cigarettes a day."***[10]

Did you know that?

NOTE: If you don't have the Core Four mastered *first,* you'll struggle in attaining your Personal Preferences.

The Personal Sanity Index
Nourishing The Body, Mind, And Spirit (Introducing The Core Four)

Reflections on Chapter 7
To get the most out of your PSI, copy this question page and document your reactions to this chapter's content. Take time to consider the questions, answer honestly, and create a journal using these pages as your writing prompts and inspiration.

1. How would you rate yourself on the Core Four regarding adequate sleep, healthy eating, weekly exercise, and maintaining personal connections?

\
\
\
\

2. Is there one or more of the Core Four that needs to become a priority for you?

\
\
\
\

3. What is your favorite form of exercise? (Dancing, walking, hiking, swimming, or something else?)

\
\
\

Chapter 8

What Do You *Really* Want?
(Discovering Personal Preferences)

This chapter is the second part of the Personal Sanity Index, where we will uncover your **Personal Preference Categories (PPC)** so you can begin/continue to reach for your goals and dreams!

Over the years, my PPC has included everything from prepping for a goal (like competing in a triathlon) to dealing with traumatic situations (like the aftermath of an earthquake), which I will expand upon later.

Tracking these *additional* daily habits has helped me reach for the skies! Literally!

You will also have that opportunity with your Index. You can link your items to something you're trying to learn or accomplish right now. For example, if your goal is to learn to play the piano, you could include "piano practice" as one of your Index items. You may not practice every day, but it's a behavior you want to engage in most days.

It could also be something that's less about a goal but is directly linked to your well-being. I've found that keeping a journal is critical for me. This chapter is where I suggest that you start one of your own.

Over the years, journaling has become a regular practice—and it's been part of my Index—even though at times it has moved out of my daily routine as other priorities have demanded my attention. You will now start tracking your Personal Preferences. Note: they will change over time.

You'll be able to achieve and *maintain success* with a simple system that includes critical, trackable behaviors to monitor progress and *variances*. After all, no one or no-thing is 100% perfect, right?

Just One Minute Every Day?

Once you create your Index (we will help you with that), it takes a minute every morning or evening.

That's it.

The Index provides a measurement tool to help you monitor where you are at the start of each day (and gives you time to think about the previous day). That's why it's a good idea to hang it somewhere you frequent each morning. Repetition and easy access will *internalize* your goals.

What If I Do It Wrong?

There is no way to fail at tracking your progress with the Index. A workbook or journal would be the companion piece, helping you map out your goals, next steps, and progress.

Let's say you have seven items in your Index—the Core Four plus three PPCs. Yesterday may have been a great day, and you scored seven out of seven. Today, your total was three, and you know why: Your neighbors had a party that interrupted your sleep.

Waking up tired, you didn't exercise, and then you grabbed a nasty convenience store breakfast burrito on your way to work. That kind of day happens to all of us. The Index will track it, and it will also show us how often we have those kinds of days. But we're not failing. We're just living life, keeping track, and learning as we go.

If you're in the middle of trying to lose weight, don't include how much you weigh each morning in your Index. Instead, track the behaviors that will help you reach your goal. Maybe that means no bedtime snacks or no sugary drinks. The Index tracks what you do. The bathroom scale will indicate whether you're achieving your goal. It's just like learning an instrument—practice makes us better; our teacher (or audience) will tell us whether we're succeeding.

What Is Your "Why?"

We can draw a direct line from how many steps we take to how many calories we burn to understand our level of fitness. But we are complicated social beings with good days and bad days and triggers that will cause us to go off track. A stressful week at work may cause a lot of late-night snacks.

The early warning *indicators* make the Index different from other goal-setting tools. Tracking them from many aspects of life helps us to recognize when and why things aren't going well in one area so we can take corrective action and avoid stress-eating kettle corn at 3 AM while watching infomercials.

The PSI helps you "weigh-in" on what you're doing while maintaining your hard-earned goals. It's the 30,000-foot overview. Track the details of your plan in a journal. If you've never had one, now's a good time to start!

Tracking The Good, The Bad, And The Ugly

The Index helps you quickly record the progress for your Core Four and Personal Preference Categories. Use the number "1" to showcase a good day of making/maintaining progress or a "0" to represent a day when you didn't.

Therefore, if you have seven categories (Core Four plus three PPCs), your optimum total goal would be a score of 7 for each day. If you see your total score at a 5 or 6, that's a good day. If you see it slipping into a 2 or 3, you're starting to move off track and you need to discover why before it becomes a bigger problem. You may be on the edge of veering off course.

In the manufacturing factory, we'd know something was wrong from the output because we'd end up with a bad batch of product. When we looked back, we realized it was caused by a specific variable, like experimenting with inputs that didn't meet our specifications.

Consider cause and effect. Input and output.

Having The Right Data

In looking at your goals, you need to know *why* something happened, but more importantly, you need to understand *what's* happening. Is there an inside or outside cause that you need to understand? (Maybe your family is staying with you for a month, or you've recently received bad news and, consequently, you're eating more and exercising less).

For me, grad school exams threw me off track. I couldn't do anything to make them go away, and I knew I wouldn't be on my A-Game for weeks. As a result, exercise and relationships would suffer. But, understanding what was going on and why—including the fact that it wouldn't persist forever—helped me to relax when my Index chart went south.

Expect Variances, Then Course Correct

I find it almost impossible not to overeat at family gatherings. Usually, it's a potluck and everybody brings their favorite dish. There's so much great food on the table, it would be rude not to try everything. And even more rude not to go back for seconds.

Oops.

Whatever the cause, a day where I don't eat within my limits gets scored as a "0" to avoid a repeat, getting me back on track. The reason we write it down is because it keeps it top of mind throughout the day to avoid repetitive self-sabotage.

Natural variability is a normal thing, not a bad thing. If one behavior is consistently off track, you can collect the data and do something about it. Life is random (and, hey, you didn't know brownies would make a celebrity appearance!).

When you expect the *occasional variance* instead of *fearing failure* (as we all do), you won't have to be obsessive about your continued progress because it's documented daily on your tracker.

The Personal Sanity Index
What Do You *Really* Want?
(Introducing Personal Preference Categories)

Reflections on Chapter 8

To get the most out of your PSI, copy this question page and document your reactions to this chapter's content. Take time to consider the questions, answer honestly, and create a journal using these pages as your writing prompts and inspiration.

1. What are your Personal Preferences (goals and dreams)? Write your answer for short-term goals here.

____

____

____

____

____

2. Write your answer to long-term goals here.

____

____

____

____

____

Chapter 9

The Key To Success: Write It Down

Studies show that routinely writing down our goals and keeping track of progress improves our productivity, leading to the best way of attaining and maintaining all that we desire. It's an essential ingredient for success in achieving goals.

Therefore, *the simple act of tracking what we eat leads to weight loss* because behavior tends to follow attention. Tracking first thing in the morning keeps our intentions top of mind throughout the day, and, as a result, we are less apt to fall prey to self-defeating actions. Indexing at the end of the day helps you put it all behind you to hit the reset button for the following day.

That's what we're helping you do with this book, the Index, the alerts on the app, and the free downloads.

You Are Priming Your Mind

After completing your Index first thing in the morning or before bed for weeks in a row, it will become automatic. You will reflexively look for the people, actions, and opportunities that will bring you closer to your goals.

As you are setting up your Index for each category, consider the critical measurements you need to take to be productive in attaining your goal. Are there related items where you must achieve "A" or "B" before you can reach "C" (your goal)? For example, is there a deadline? Are there people or things that will become a distraction?

When I knew I wanted to race competitively, I started by mapping out a training plan and making sure I had the clothing and shoes to be successful at running (A). Then I shared my dream with friends and family so they would respect my schedule (B), and I used the race date as my deadline (C).

A little prep work made all the difference.

But This Is Where I Went Off Track!

There's a reason I've included "personal connections" as one of the Core Four. Neglecting this category was a *big failure* in one of my early relationships when I put all of my energy—to the point of obsession—into achieving and maintaining goals by focusing on the other categories, and I left this one out *entirely.*

Years later, I realized it was a desperate attempt to keep myself on track, but I was self-centered and ultimately sabotaged the relationship. That one's on me, and I disappointed someone I loved. Unfortunately, I had to learn the hard way not to do that again.

If I'd had a stronger sense of "we" rather than "me," maybe the relationship wouldn't have ended. My suggestion: Don't build a self-isolating checklist because interpersonal connections are essential. Put things in your Index that engage you with your community.

The good news? Today, I'm happily married and have a daughter who inspires me every day. And I continue to cultivate new friendships while sustaining old ones because great relationships are another thing that has kept me sane.

I attribute a lot of my successes to surrounding myself with the right people (and knowing when to get away from the wrong ones).

Don't Let It Happen To You

Looking back, once I got sober, I joined new groups and made friends who had like-minded goals, hobbies, and pastimes. It has made all the difference for me. I've learned that an essential part of maintaining my mental and emotional health includes having a support system, and I've exchanged going to the bars at night with having brunch with friends after a morning run.

So, who is your support team? Maybe it's a combination of family, colleagues, and friends. I suggest preserving those meaningful relationships by tracking them as part of your Core Four.

The Personal Sanity Index
The Key To Success: Write It Down

Reflections on Chapter 9

To get the most out of your PSI, copy this question page and document your reactions to this chapter's content. Take time to consider the questions, answer honestly, and create a journal using these pages as your writing prompts and inspiration.

1. In the past, have you expected variances? How will you lean on the Index to track them as part of a natural process in accomplishing your next goal?

____

____

____

2. You've been documenting your goals. (Good job!) In doing so, have you realized there is an A or B step that needs to happen before you can work on your ultimate goal of C? Itemize them here and give them dates for completion to keep you on track.

____

____

____

3. Who do you have as personal connections (family, friends, mentors, therapists, counselors, colleagues)? Is it a good time to expand this list by asking someone new out for a friendly chat? Is there a group, event, or activity you could join to expand your network?

____

____

____

Chapter 10

Are You Looking For The Best Version Of Yourself?

I have a friend named Tom who spends a lot of time thinking about how his life could be if things had worked out differently. He believes he can't quit a job he hates because of the paycheck and benefits. But he's miserable working where he is.

Unfortunately, this is the plight of a lot of us, whether we're stuck in an undesirable job or a lackluster relationship—or an unachieved dream is haunting us.

At the age of 40, Tom doesn't realize he's living in a constant state of depression. His anxiety is always bubbling just under the surface because his belief that *life hasn't been kind to him* overflows into everything he touches, including his relationships with family and friends.

This belief taxes his health because he's always anxious, as if holding his breath, waiting for the weekends, holidays, and vacations from his 9-to-5 grind. When Sunday night comes along, he finds himself staring down the barrel of what seems like another Monday through Friday prison sentence.

A darkness casts a shadow over him as he thinks about clocking in the next day.

Doesn't He Realize He's The Only One Who Can Fix This?

Tom thinks he's hiding his sadness because he masks it by putting on a happy face whenever he spends time with friends and family. At his daughter's insistence, Tom went to the doctor last week for the depression he's been denying. The extra 25 pounds he's packed on is a visible side effect.

His family notices his mood, and his daughter Wendy is afraid he's *wishing his life away,* only living for weekends and vacations. When they discuss it with him, he always makes excuses about why he won't consider a change that could make him happier.

Dad's Happy Being Miserable

Do you know someone like Tom? Someone who is unhappy with a certain part of their life, but refuses to *take action* even though he or she is the only one who can change it?

There's a big difference between *surviving* the day-to-day and *thriving.* Lots of us are happy just to be "okay," getting by with the bare minimums as we try to claw our way to the top, holding on by our fingernails and hoping not to fall back into the pit.

When Is Enough, Enough?

Your Personal Sanity Index will not be able to find you a new job, but you can use it to evaluate, build, and monitor the steps needed to improve your situation—and help you to figure out what isn't working. Then, you'll formulate a plan in your workbook/journal, documenting the steps you need to take to improve your situation by tracking them in your Index.

Are You Living In A Negative State?

It's tough trying to get people to stop living in their heads and take action to make real, lasting changes. In most situations, we have a choice *but believe we don't.* I'm saddened by the number of people who think they're stuck in a relationship, job, or other situation when there are other options out there.

Are you living in a negative environment of someone else's making—or your own—without knowing it? I did that to myself for a decade, sure that I wouldn't be able to sleep or cope with other humans without alcohol.

Even in recovery, it took years of introspection and a newfound awareness about my thought patterns to make sure I wasn't self-sabotaging regularly. In fact, when an incredible job opportunity came my way, I almost didn't consider it because I was comfortable in a position I'd occupied for more than a decade.

A friend of mine called me out on my lack of response, accusing me of being complacent and being happy by *coasting*. I was angry at him at the time, but I thought about it, and I'm so glad he challenged me.

I almost missed the opportunity of a lifetime! My current role in teaching at the University of Michigan and leading the Entrepreneurial Studies program has been the highlight of my career. I've helped many students over the years by encouraging them to follow their dreams of launching a company.

My lesson? We *all* need to watch out for self-sabotaging behaviors that limit us from reaching our full potential so we can make a positive impact on the world! The Index has helped me take control of what I can.

What Worked For Me

Years ago, after rehab, I got some additional counseling, and I've been able to be *kinder* to myself, no longer making decisions based on fear. Instead, I look at the bigger picture: *What isn't working? What would I rather have?* Then I make a plan to start moving forward the next day.

Being kinder to myself helps me to be more considerate of others.

A significant change in perspective came when I adjusted my goals to allow for *gradual* change—not overnight miracles.

After the move to Vancouver, I started training as a runner, hoping to compete in marathons *someday*. At the time, it seemed like a far-reaching, almost ridiculous goal. I also discovered a local karate club. The intensity of the training kicked my butt, but I loved being part of a group of people working hard to get better at doing something they loved.

I also had my Index tracker, and I used the discipline that came with the training to help me proactively *live my life on purpose,* with a plan for goals and the flexibility to adjust and pursue new interests and opportunities as they developed. After spending so many years feeling like crap, I discovered that getting healthy was pivotal to peaceful living.

I knew I was finally on my way to something amazing!

Feeling Strong (And Sometimes Bruised)

In 1992, at the age of 27, I trained for my first 10K: the Pacific Spirit Run in British Columbia. Whenever I think back on achieving that goal, I remember a steep hill at the 7K mark. As I struggled and considered the consequences of failing, I realized it was a metaphor for all the training I'd done preparing for that day.

A First Nations Tribe owned the park, and they must have known what a feat climbing that hill would be because they strategically placed drummers at its base. The drumbeat got louder and louder as I chugged along to the boom-boom-boom beat, not allowing fear to win. Even though the "run" felt more like a crawl on that hill, I continued to push myself, and I'm glad I did.

I finished the race in the middle of the pack with sweat on my brow and a smile on my face. To this day, whenever I hear a rhythmic drumbeat, it takes me back to the victorious feeling of that day. Optimism was beginning to win the battle against pessimism between my ears. I was hopeful for my future, believing I could take on challenges and win the game that addiction stacked against me for so many years.

My Transformation

Once I was feeling better, I knew I wanted more out of life than just the basic Core Four. So, I allowed myself to dream about my long-term future.

I asked myself: *What isn't working for me?* Soon, this became a new mantra as I was looking for continuous personal improvement.

Sometimes It's Obvious

After running my first half-marathon, I had a *significant* setback. I sustained a knee injury and lived with a lot of physical pain. Fortunately, I was able to rebound quickly because I was young and healthy.

After physical therapy concluded, I talked to other runners who had been through the same thing and I decided to train for a triathlon instead, hoping it would be kinder on my knees while enabling me to strengthen other parts of my body.

I love a good challenge!

I read a book called *Triathloning For Ordinary Mortals* (by Steve Jones) and used some of his tips. That book, combined with the Index, helped me train, reach my goals, and prep for the event.

In 1993, at the age of 28, I participated in the Vancouver International Triathlon (swim, bike, run) and was proud to finish in the middle of the field!

I was using the Index to keep myself on track with my studies as an MBA student and my training. Over the years, I've realized that if I'm training for a specific goal with a *date* in mind—like a karate competition—it's easier to stick to a workout schedule if the building blocks of my day-to-day (the Core Four) are taken care of consistently.

Getting Off Track — It Happens Sometimes

Working my way through two rounds of grad school came with specific challenges. Healthy eating with an adequate sleep schedule and daily exercise was often put on the back burner as I wrote papers and studied for finals and midterms.

Back then, I saw significant declines that could have quickly become *excuses,* taking me completely off track—especially with my sobriety. It was a time when I could have thrown the Index out the window, but I didn't because I'd experienced so much success!

This was when I started to use the Index to help cope with challenging situations. Knowing I was in a busy period of work or study enabled me to make sense of the low daily scores I was seeing on my checklist. It also motivated me to do better the next day—seeking progress, not perfection.

Yes, I treated myself to celebratory ice cream after exams were over, but I'd been counting the days when I could get *back on track*, realizing the Index was like leaning on a good friend. I knew that starting to regain my healthy eating while catching up on sleep (and, therefore, sanity) was only a day away.

Another Milestone

In 1993, after graduating with my MBA, my girlfriend told me she'd like to move to Japan to study the language, culture, and tourism industry (her major area of study). I was ready for an adventure and was excited about the prospect of learning *traditional* karate from the masters.

It was time to let her lead the way.

We both taught English while we were there. I joined a dojo and earned my black belt in Shotokan.

It was an exciting adventure, but after a year, we went our separate ways. As I mentioned earlier, I believe the split came because of my obsession with my own goals (instead of our relationship). I over-indexed on self-development, discovering new things, and maintaining my progress, but I didn't include the people close to me.

It was a wake-up call.

Shaking Things Up

In 1995, soon after we separated, a massive earthquake hit Kobe, Japan, where I was living. It was 7.2 on the Richter scale, and buildings and bridges crumbled like dust. When it happened, at 5:00 AM, I was in my apartment sleeping.

It was terrifying.

The noise and violence of the earthquake were incredible, and I was lucky that my building was relatively new construction built on a hilltop. Older buildings, especially those on the soft soil near the coast, suffered much more damage. The residents of those structures weren't so fortunate.

I experienced an unsettling time after that and noticed an underlying state of anxiety and depression that was unlike anything I'd experienced before. Countless aftershocks continued to trigger me. When I felt the ground shake, I'd wonder if I was in the midst of a small tremor or about to become a victim of another big quake. Even the vibrations caused by a passing truck were enough to trigger my anxiety.

It was a rough way to live—and I know I wasn't the only one going through life in that state of constant stress.

Living In Survival Mode

For quite some time, Kobe's electricity and running water were shut off, making day-to-day living difficult. I moved into a friend's house in a nearby city and slept on the floor for weeks, returning to my apartment later for clothes and food.

Coming back to the scene created physical and mental aftershocks as I felt adrenaline shooting through my body, creating an uncomfortable and uncontrollable panic racing through my heart. When I went back to my apartment, I felt like I was holding my breath while diving underwater because "home" did not feel like a safe space.

I realized I'd have to learn how to calm the *internal* tremors next.

The *old me* would have let the trauma become an excuse to feel sorry for myself and return to the bottle. But using the Index, and what I call "next" habits, helped me to survive.

When my teaching contract ended at the end of the academic year, I returned to Vancouver to begin my Ph.D. studies. I was also able to share my newly developed martial arts skills working as a volunteer instructor at a local karate club. I was back in beautiful British Columbia, teaching and learning, the two things to which I have devoted my life ever since.

It was good to be *home.*

Hidden Secrets

Later, I realized my exaggerated response to feeling any low-frequency vibration was a form of post-traumatic stress disorder (PTSD). It helped me understand what was happening to me and why certain triggers would incite my fight-or-flight response. I'm fortunate I made it through, but the event and the lingering effects were a danger to my sanity.

I was lucky I had the Index, and I relied on it repeatedly. It proved to be a valuable tool and I believe I would *not have been able to stay sober without it.* One reason it works is similar to the magic of keeping a journal. Once you write something down—or plot it on a chart—you can let it go. A lot of resentment, regret, and anxiety can persist in our minds because our thoughts keep chasing each other in circles with no way to stop.

That's the secret to using the Personal Sanity Index: Hand it over to the tracker every morning or evening and enjoy your life because you've created a customized plan where everything's covered.

The PSI has got your back.

The Personal Sanity Index
Are You Looking For The Best Version Of Yourself?

Reflections on Chapter 10

To get the most out of your PSI, copy this question page and document your reactions to this chapter's content. Take time to consider the questions, answer honestly, and create a journal using these pages as your writing prompts and inspiration.

1. Is an unachieved dream haunting you? If so, what is it, and how will you track it on the Index?

____

____

____

2. Do you believe life has been unkind to you? Do you think life is difficult? Do you see how these thoughts may be keeping you from realizing your dreams? Explain.

____

____

____

3. Are you kind to yourself? Have you forgiven yourself and others for perceived past misdeeds? Do you see how these thoughts may be keeping you from realizing your dreams? Explain.

____

____

____

Chapter 11

Are You On A Quest To Live A Better Life?

When I initially created my Personal Sanity Index, I found certain things in the Core Four (like healthy eating and exercise) came naturally to me. Other items (like personal connections) continued to be something I'd have to work on *daily*.

You may also find that some categories need more attention than others.

I got into a groove *protecting* these four categories, noting that sleep was no longer a source of anxiety for me. Once I got my equilibrium back after rehab and started making better choices—like not staying out late—sleep became a welcome friend.

What a relief!

I was on a quest to discover the best version of myself and *make my life more fulfilling.*

The Ups And Downs

If you want to embrace everything the days ahead will bring—including the challenges and the triumphs—you will love the Personal Sanity Index.

Start by documenting and protecting your Core Four while tracking them daily and allowing for slight variances. Let's face it, it's not always possible to get a good night's sleep, and that's why this system allows for not-perfect outcomes!

I've found that if we don't get our basic human needs met, we don't have the capacity to accomplish other *loftier* goals. Regarding *your* Personal Preferences, allow me to offer shortcuts as I explain my best practices.

Let's Make It Easy!

In the beginning, I noticed that daily tracking with **weekly monitoring** worked to help me focus on my priority—maintaining my sobriety—and, in turn, my sanity. When I felt myself at risk of backsliding, I focused my attention on two things: *behaviors* that were taking me off-track, and what I knew I could do for immediate *course correction like Quality Assurance in the factory.*

For example, when I felt myself thinking about drinking instead of living sober, I knew I needed *grounding actions* that I listed in my journal.

I'd ask myself:
1. Did I go to an AA meeting recently?
2. Did I meditate recently?
3. Did I talk to my sponsor?

Once I started implementing these behaviors, I quickly got back on track. Over time, I've realized my PPCs have evolved. Yours will change too. As a result, you'll be able to include loftier goals in your plans.

More on that later.

Consider Your Personal Preference Categories

Now that we've covered the basics, let's create **your customized plan**. Start by identifying the *best version of yourself.* When are you at your best? Make a list that includes 3-5 things that you want to achieve or maintain.

If you don't know when you're at your best, ask your friends and family. They know what makes you happy and when you are feeling joyful and complete.

So often, we don't allow ourselves to dream, or we overlook the simple things of life. Other times, we think we don't *need* or even *deserve* to attain individual goals because we're busy caring for others, growing our businesses, or we're worried about health or financial issues.

But there's nothing wrong with each of us—as individuals—going after what makes our hearts *sing*. Isn't that why we're here?

Excuses are no longer an option!

The good news? Your PSI (with PPC) will help you get there.

The Personal Sanity Index
Are You On A Quest To Live A Better Life?

Reflections on Chapter 11

To get the most out of your PSI, copy this question page and document your reactions to this chapter's content. Take time to consider the questions, answer honestly, and create a journal using these pages as your writing prompts and inspiration.

1. What are your best grounding exercises in times of stress?

____

____

____

2. What makes your heart sing?

____

____

____

____

____

3. When you allow yourself to dream about a bright future, what comes up? What changes will you need to make?

____

____

____

Chapter 12

Realize What You Can And Can't Control

One of the nicest compliments I've received from friends and colleagues who have used the PSI is that the Index helps them feel they are gaining control over an issue that is bothering (even tormenting) them, helping them cope with the unpredictability of life.

As I am writing this book, we are in the midst of the COVID-19 pandemic. Because of the peculiar nature of this virus, entire states (representing most of the country) have been shut down. Businesses have closed and hospitals are at maximum capacity.

As I've watched my newsfeed around the clock, I've noticed I was feeling anxious during the day and wasn't sleeping well. Soon, my Index started sliding into low numbers. Once I realized the virus wasn't going away anytime soon, I knew I needed to make a plan.

Over the years, our bodies have evolved to deal with sudden stress; however, we haven't adapted to coping with the weight of continuous, *unrelenting* stress. Adrenaline can be our friend if we need to get out of a dangerous situation quickly, but constant production of the stress hormone, cortisol, can cause significant harm to our physical and mental well-being over time.

Three factors contribute to how much we can endure, day in and day out. They are uncertainty, lack of control, and newness.

1. Uncertainty. When we don't know what's going to happen next or how or when things will change, anxiety can take hold. For example, as we navigate the daily news regarding the number of COVID infections, increasing death rates, and announcements about our state's shelter-in-place quarantines, we are living in a prolonged, heightened state of uncertainty. The effects of living this way can be cumulative and long-lasting, affecting our mental, emotional and physical health.

2. Lack of control. Even when things are changing rapidly, we can cope as long as we feel certain events or aspects of our lives are within our span of control. But when businesses are forced to close for public health reasons, control is taken away. We don't know when a state of emergency will lift or how life will look once the pandemic is over. As everyone adjusts to a *lack of control* and a "new normal," mental health professionals warn against the anxiety and depression caused by this outbreak.

3. Newness. The "novel" virus is something we haven't seen before, so we can't draw on past treatments or courses of action as a sure fix. For some, an adrenaline reaction occurs every time we leave the safety of our homes to go grocery shopping and risk exposure to the virus. The long-term effects include a constant cortisol release, causing people to stress eat, stress drink, and become depressed and anxious. Perversely, this reaction can do a great deal of damage to the immune system, making us more susceptible to the virus.

Understanding these three causes of stress helped me cope. Knowing what I could and couldn't control was the first step.

You *Can* Control How You're Living, Even If You *Can't* Control Life

I grabbed my journal and started marking these things down in two columns: *What I Can Control* and *What I Can't Control.*

I wanted to have a proactive plan in place so I didn't feel like a victim through resistance or denial (which definitely won't keep my family safe) or passive-aggressive behaviors. After surviving the Japanese earthquake that shook my life, I didn't want to come out of the pandemic with another bout of PTSD, which can rewire one's brain.

Been there. Done that. Got the t-shirt.

Living In A Negative Vs. Positive State

I'm certain there will be many people who will have a PTSD diagnosis during (or after) the pandemic, especially those who have suffered through the loss of loved ones and their own battles with the virus. None of us is immune to mental health challenges any more than we are to novel pathogens. I knew turning on the cortisol production would compromise the immune system, which is essential in combating the virus. I wanted all the protection I could muster for my family and me, so I found a way to relax by educating myself as much as I could.

In my daily Index, I tracked a new Personal Preference Category: "Manage Risk." Then I created a checklist of things I could do regularly to ensure success. These included limiting trips into crowded places, like grocery stores, wearing a mask, frequent hand-washing, and other measures known to minimize the risk of infection. It's impossible to eliminate risk from our daily lives, but there's no reason not to take an active role in reducing it.

I put a plan in place and calmed down. Developing a strategy always makes me feel like I have an aspect of control, even when things are scary. When the governors asked us to shelter in place, I knew we were doing it to protect ourselves until we understood more about the virus and how it spread.

I used my journal and the Index to get me through a tough time while protecting my health, my family, and my sobriety.

Other long-term stressors can be managed with the PSI. Because worry interferes with sleep, it can also contribute to depression, which can lead to unhealthy eating. Have you heard of the "Freshman 15?" In 2020, it translated into the "COVID 15" because so many people packed on weight by staying home from work and stress eating. And drinking.

I shared this information with my colleagues, and they used it to gain control in reducing the stress that comes with the unpredictability of life.

The Personal Sanity Index
Realize What You Can And Can't Control

Reflections on Chapter 12

To get the most out of your PSI, copy this question page and document your reactions to this chapter's content. Take time to consider the questions, answer honestly, and create a journal using these pages as your writing prompts and inspiration.

1. Are you suffering from unrelenting stress? Is something bothering or tormenting you?

____

____

____

____

____

____

2. Think about a time in the past when you've gone through a hard time. Have you made good decisions most of the time? What can you add to your Index tracker to ensure success?

____

____

____

____

____

____

3. Use the chart below to list what you can and cannot control as it relates to a trouble spot in your life. Look at the lists you've created and make a plan for personal improvement with specific dates. Take steps to accomplish something every day, week, and month.

What I CAN control.   **What I CANNOT control.**

Section Three

Creating Your PSI: How To Use It

*"Real change, enduring change,
happens one step at a time."*
— Ruth Bader Ginsburg

Chapter 13

Build Your PSI Index Tracker
(In Six Easy Steps)

Now that you understand the basics, creating your Personal Sanity Index should be a fun exercise because you get to dream about all of the cool stuff you want to show up in your life! Once you have mastered the Core Four, your focus can move to other parts of your life (Personal Preferences), creating a ripple effect of success.

Yes, there will be some trial and error, but you will start by answering the three simple questions below and documenting them in your journal. Then we will show you how to build your Index tracker with templates on pages 76-78. Use your answers to guide your choice of Personal Preferences to make sure you're tracking the right things every day.

1. Ask yourself these three questions:
a) What isn't working for me? What upsets me, makes me anxious, or isn't giving me a return on my investment of time or money? Stop reading and take this exercise seriously because everything else hinges on this question. Use the next 10 minutes to write the answer(s) in your workbook or journal. Your list may be short or long—it doesn't matter.

b) What would I rather have? This is the time to consider all of your options! Dream a little dream. Or a big one! That nagging feeling is there for a reason. It's trying to get your attention. *Honor it.* Answer this question then watch your life change in the next several months!

c) What needs to happen (repeatedly) to succeed? Think about the steps you need to take—and keep taking—to get you from where you are to where you want to be. Creating a plan is critical and the Index will help you get there.

You may have instant answers, or you may have to stop and assess your current situation because several of your responses are tied together or they overlap. Think about items you may be *overlooking* and things that are *obvious*. Write each one down and create a list of 5–10 items. Use the list below to get started.

Do you need a change in one or more of these areas?
- Social life (scheduling time with friends, enjoying fun adventures, and taking vacations)
- Home life (right-sizing, making home improvements, moving to another neighborhood)
- Financial (improving your credit score, asking for a promotion, starting a savings/retirement plan)
- Spiritual (starting a daily/weekly practice, joining an online community)
- Career (pursuing a better job, taking classes, starting your own business)
- Relationships (finding new friends/romance, ending what doesn't bring you joy)
- Health and well-being (taking care of your emotional, mental, and physical well-being)

Use these or come up with three to five categories of your own to use as goals with a timeline. As mentioned earlier, eating well should be included in the foundational Core Four with a plan in your workbook/journal for healthy eating and exercise, whereas you would include the daily activities associated with, say, writing a book in the additional Personal Preference Categories.

2. Assess the changes you want to make and give them a timeline. Document the reasons *why* you must achieve this goal: A) what problems will it solve? B) how will it make life better? Then give it a nickname (for simplicity) for the tracker. Make sure it's specific and has a target date.

For example, if you want to spend a year in Italy, you may break that down into smaller goals, such as saving money and learning Italian. Each of those can then be tied to specific behaviors that you would include in your Index. Just as sleeping well is the behavior associated with starting each day well-rested, you need to think about the actions that will result in financial savings and language acquisition. Is it something you want to do a year from now or five years in the future? The time horizon will help you shape the things you need to do and how often they need to happen.

3. Decide on the next steps. Document the progress you've made (in your journal/workbook) and assess whether you're on the right track!

If saving money to get to Italy is part of your plan, an Index item might be as simple as putting $10 in a coffee jar. After a year, that would add up to $520, if you did it once a week, or $1,825 if you did it every other day! Just like every Index item, it's a desirable behavior that leads to a positive outcome.

But if you don't make it every time, that's the normal (imperfect) part of being human. The goal of "saving money" is too general to work on a daily checklist. Putting $10 in a jar is specific, and you can score it as "Yes" you did or "No" you didn't on a daily/weekly basis.

The same applies to learning a language. If you put "Learn Italian" on your checklist, you'd be continually failing until you finally reached your goal. But "Practiced Italian for 30 minutes" or "Listened to 'News in Slow Italian'" can be tracked.

That's why we suggest "Exercise" as an item in the Core Four rather than "Get in Shape." One is a long-term goal. The Index is about daily, clearly defined behavior.

If you want to become a better cook, for example, make a list of steps that will affect your progress (taking a class, baking on Sundays). Then break each one down into steps and write them in your journal to help you measure your success.

There is one word of caution I want to mention: Do not confuse **input** or "behavior" (like trying new recipes) for **output** or "result" (like baking three types of delicious, flawless bread). It's the **positive behaviors** that are important.

Similar to Quality Assurance, you need to identify the right inputs, then include them in your workbook. For example, if we define the critical inputs of baking bread, we will note the following in our workbook:

- The temperature of the preheated oven must be 450 degrees
- The temp of the water must be 90–110 degrees
- The dough should rise until it has doubled in size

If all of our known inputs are accurate, then we'll have a consistent loaf day after day—year after year. But we also know that ovens and different batches of flour can vary, and we will grow to learn how much *variance* we can have before the results go off-target.

If you take all measurements at the beginning and end of each shift on any given day, most items won't be perfect. There could be a plus or minus one degree in the oven or a variance in the gluten levels.

However, if more than one or two of these items are off their limit, the bread will be undercooked, flat, or burned. Or, it could rise beyond what it should. That's why it's a good idea to always start with the core inputs, and if everything's right, we'll have a good product.

Note: Only track the *critical things* that make a difference. For example, the temperature of the oven is a vital element, whereas the level of lighting in the bakery is not.

There are things in life that are similar to making bread. We need to track sleep, food, exercise, connections, and personal goals or we won't be at our consistent best. By monitoring the key inputs, we can ensure the best outputs to create our best lives.

It's about getting all the clutter cleaned up in your head so you can get to the goal.

4. Build your tracker. Create a spreadsheet (with the free app, downloadable PDF at personalsanityindex.com, or use a spreadsheet app) and start tracking behaviors over *the next week*. Use this time to collect data without judgment and don't worry about being perfect.

At the end of this chapter we've included:

- a PSI worksheet with the Core Four and samples of PPCs to choose from (including Basic, Active, Spiritual, and Recovery)
- an example of a completed PSI worksheet
- a blank PSI Worksheet (to get you started)

5. Use it daily. Once you input your customized info, *it only takes a minute every day!* Humans are highly visual creatures, so print it and position it at eye level somewhere you frequent each morning or evening (like the fridge, the bathroom, or your home office).

Track your Core Four items and Personal Preference Categories (three to five items) daily by using a "1" in each category where you achieved your desired behavior (e.g., got a good night's sleep). Use a "0" where you didn't. It's really that simple.

If you have seven categories, your **best score for each day totals 7.** If it becomes a 4 or lower, you need to identify what is affecting your score. For example, I've noticed that traveling can affect my scores because sleeping (jet lag), eating, and exercising shifts with my new environment. Disruptions in life will show up as disruptions on your daily Index score. If you know it's a temporary situation, allow for the variance and get back on track ASAP.

How? The next day, you *prioritize* sleep, ask the hotel staff about healthy eating in the city, and walk to those restaurants and other attractions when possible. Then you will soon see the numbers rising in your Index again.

If you're at home and things are normal and your Index numbers are plummeting, you need to ask yourself why, make adjustments, and track it for the next couple of days.

NOTE: You can use the PSI App as your home screen to keep your goals top of mind. Open it up each day to track the previous day's results— schedule alerts and reminders to help you remember until it becomes automatic.

6. Be aware of downward trends. This step is tougher because you don't always know what's wrong. If you see your daily total getting lower for more than a couple of days, it's worth investing some time to figure out why. For example, has it been several days since you've slept well or found time to exercise? Is there an obvious cause for the decline (e.g., you're traveling and it's hard to eat/sleep/exercise well) or is this just a temporary blip that you will easily bounce back from in the coming days? Don't feel guilty about what you did yesterday. Don't let it derail you. You've got today—record it. Then do the *next right thing.*

The emphasis shouldn't be on daily change, but daily *behaviors.* By focusing on easily adjustable behaviors, we aren't caught in a cycle of shame when we don't see the kind of progress we expect.

The magic is in the *positive change seen over time,* enabling us to be patient and kind to ourselves.

Choosing Your Personal Preference Categories

When you're at your best, you're moving toward the things that are life-affirming *for you.* Your list won't be the same as anyone else's—and that's okay—because you are unique.

For example, ask yourself: **At the end of a great day, what are the things you did that made it so good?** Did you have quiet time to read? Did you go dancing? Listen to music? Play with your dog? (These are PPCs.)

Also, add the **things you did to take care of yourself:** Did you sleep eight hours? Eat a healthy dinner? Have coffee with a friend? Walk in nature? (These are the Core Four.)

I've found my chances of relapsing were *really low* on a day jammed with my favorite activities. But if I didn't pay attention to my Personal Preference Categories, I was at risk. In your list, include items that bring you joy and nourishment. They should be things that you *could* do every day, but don't feel that you *have* to do *all* of them every day.

Achieving Peak Performance

What do you want to accomplish over the next 6–12 months and which actions will get you to your goal? If you've already achieved your goal, you want to track habits that will help you *continue* your progress.

Break each one down into a plan with small, manageable goals that you track in your workbook. Then, take steps each day to achieve or maintain your hard-earned goal and track it in the Index.

For example, if you've decided to write your memoir, you may want to use *time spent writing* or *number of pages written* as a measurement of your daily commitment and progress. If you hope to spend two hours a day writing or producing two pages of text, both of those activities represent clear, trackable behaviors. As with all items that we choose as PPCs, the simpler and more easily observable they are (i.e., you did it or you didn't) the better they'll work as components of your Index.

Choose Your Personal Preference Categories (PPCs)

I recommend including the Core Four in your Index, then adding up to three Personal Preference Categories (PPCs) with the possibility of seven items on your daily checklist.

Here are your Core Four and suggestions for PPCs based on different profiles/priorities:

The Core Four	**Nickname**
Did I sleep well last night (quantity and quality)?	Sleep
Did I eat well today (quantity and quality)?	Eat
Did I exercise today?	Exercise
Did I spend time with people who matter to me?	People

BASIC Personal Preference Categories	**Nickname**
Did I find something to be grateful for today?	Gratitude
Did I learn something new about the world?	Learning
Did I take quiet time for myself?	Peace

ACTIVE Personal Preference Categories	**Nickname**
Did I stretch?	Stretch
Did I stay hydrated?	Hydrate
Did I try something new?	Novelty

SPIRITUAL Personal Preference Categories	**Nickname**
Did I find something to be grateful for today?	Gratitude
Did I make time for prayer (or meditation)?	Prayer
Did I help someone else today?	Helping

RECOVERY Personal Preference Categories	**Nickname**
Did I attend a meeting?	Meeting
Did I connect with my sponsor?	Sponsor
Did I write in my journal?	Journal

Figure 1

Example of Completed PSI Chart

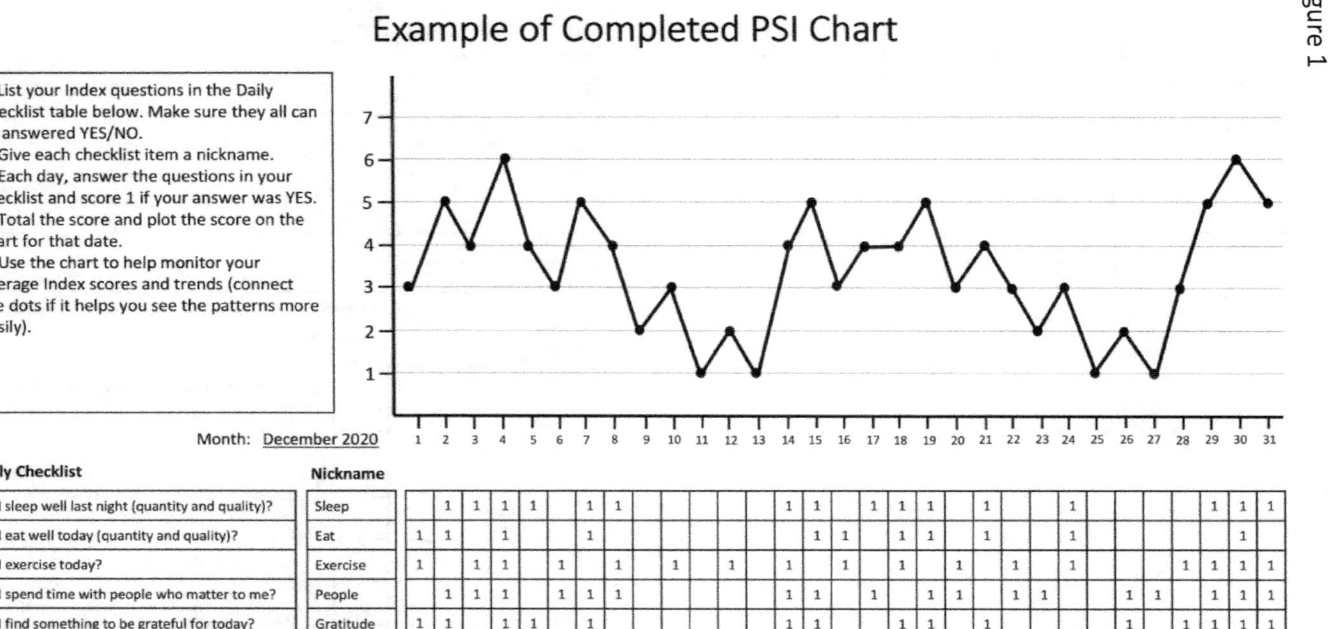

1. List your Index questions in the Daily Checklist table below. Make sure they all can be answered YES/NO.
2. Give each checklist item a nickname.
3. Each day, answer the questions in your checklist and score 1 if your answer was YES.
4. Total the score and plot the score on the chart for that date.
5. Use the chart to help monitor your average Index scores and trends (connect the dots if it helps you see the patterns more easily).

Month: <u>December 2020</u>

Daily Checklist

Daily Checklist	Nickname	1	2	3	4	5	6	7	8	9	10	11	12	13	14	15	16	17	18	19	20	21	22	23	24	25	26	27	28	29	30	31
Did I sleep well last night (quantity and quality)?	Sleep		1	1	1	1		1	1						1	1		1	1	1		1			1					1	1	1
Did I eat well today (quantity and quality)?	Eat	1	1		1			1								1	1		1	1		1			1						1	
Did I exercise today?	Exercise	1		1	1		1		1		1		1		1		1		1		1		1		1				1	1	1	1
Did I spend time with people who matter to me?	People		1	1	1		1	1	1						1	1		1		1	1		1	1			1	1		1	1	1
Did I find something to be grateful for today?	Gratitude	1	1		1	1		1							1	1			1	1		1					1		1	1	1	1
Did I learn something new about the world?	Learning		1	1	1	1	1		1	1	1	1					1	1				1		1							1	1
Did I take quiet time for myself?	Quiet					1		1		1	1		1	1		1		1		1	1		1			1			1	1		
	TOTAL	3	5	4	6	4	3	5	4	2	3	1	2	1	4	5	3	4	4	5	3	4	3	2	3	1	2	1	3	5	6	5
Date:		1	2	3	4	5	6	7	8	9	10	11	12	13	14	15	16	17	18	19	20	21	22	23	24	25	26	27	28	29	30	31

Figure 2

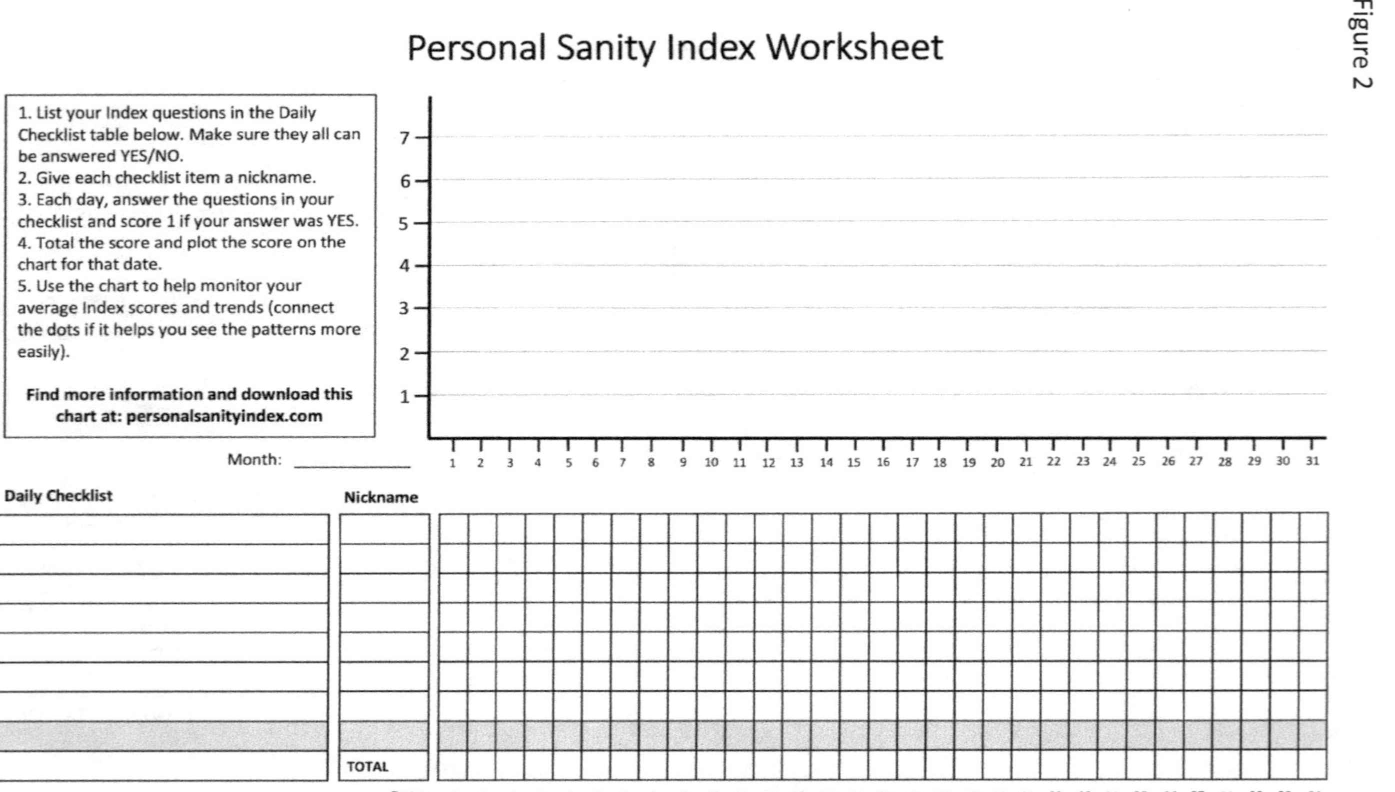

Personal Sanity Index Worksheet
1. List your Index questions in the Daily Checklist table below. Make sure they all can be answered YES/NO.
2. Give each checklist item a nickname.
3. Each day, answer the questions in your checklist and score 1 if your answer was YES.
4. Total the score and plot the score on the chart for that date.
5. Use the chart to help monitor your average Index scores and trends (connect the dots if it helps you see the patterns more easily).
Find more information and download this chart at: personalsanityindex.com
Month:
Daily Checklist
Nickname
TOTAL
Date:

The Personal Sanity Index
Build Your PSI Index Tracker (In Six Easy Steps)

Reflections on Chapter 13
To get the most out of your PSI, copy this question page and document your reactions to this chapter's content. Take time to consider the questions, answer honestly, and create a journal using these pages as your writing prompts and inspiration.

1. In your current day today, what isn't working for you?

____

____

____

2. What would you rather have?

____

____

____

3. Do you need a change in your social life, home life, financial situation, spiritual practices, career, relationships, health? Explain.

____

____

____

____

4. How will these changes make life better?

____

____

____

____

____

5. What is your timeline?

____

____

____

____

____

6. What steps will you take to ensure success?

____

____

____

____

____

Chapter 14

Assessing Your Progress

The Index Worksheet provides a visual record of where you are each day, relative to your ideal best self. As weeks go by, ask yourself if managing your goals has become easier. If your answer is yes, the Index is working and you can now think about adding other categories.

If you are anything like me, you will love checking off those goals while reaching for the next one!

Think about getting weekly averages:

- Do you feel better this week over last week?
- Do you see a new, positive trend that came from a new habit?
- Are you moving closer to your goal?

Creating Balance With Your Index

Here are some tips to make the construction of your Index easy and optimized to work best for you.

- Build the Index slowly. Try a couple of weeks with just the Core Four or with a single Personal Preference Category. Add additional PPC items at a pace that works for you. I recommend three to five PPCs for a total Index tally of seven to nine items. Over time, you may want to retire some things and add others to keep within the seven-to-nine range.

- If you find there are things you don't need to track because you do them naturally, take them off your list. For example, if you've added meditation as a PPC but you've meditated every day for the last ten years and are unlikely to ever miss a day, add something that's more aspirational (and more variable).

- Make sure most of your items are independent of each other, so if one thing goes wrong, it's not a house of cards. If all seven things depend on getting a good night's sleep, for example, then other elements will be affected and your daily score will be overly sensitive to a single measure of well-being. Wellness has many components. If you can select items that capture some of these different dimensions, you'll be tracking a wider range of indicators and getting a more complete picture of each day. The Core Four is weighted toward physical well-being (because it's so foundational). For your PPCs, look to areas such as financial, spiritual, emotional, or intellectual to track a broader view of how you're doing each day.

The Personal Sanity Index
Assessing Your Progress

Reflections on Chapter 14

To get the most out of your PSI, copy this question page and document your reactions to this chapter's content. Take time to consider the questions, answer honestly, and create a journal using these pages as your writing prompts and inspiration.

1. Start your Index with the Core Four and one PPC. Do you already know which one(s) you'll choose? List them here.

Chapter 15

Does A Part Of Your Life Feel Like It's Out Of Control?

You know what you want to accomplish. Whether it's an aspiration, a work-in-progress, or you're already across the finish line, the Index is *the process* that will keep you from backsliding.

After I came home from Japan, I realized I needed more high-quality social connections. I'd been away for years, and it felt like I was starting all over again. In fact, I was. It was the beginning of four years of grad school with new professors, new classmates, and new challenges. It was time to change some of my PPCs and an opportunity to rely on the foundation provided by the Core Four.

"Reverse Culture Shock"

Returning to Vancouver, I expected to feel right at home, but I experienced something experts call "reverse culture shock" from being immersed in another culture.

As a result, I'd find things that didn't upset me before were now downright *unacceptable.* For example, as a grad student, I didn't have a car, so I took the bus a lot. Buses in the US and Canada are, shall we say, more *flexible* in their arrival times than Japanese public transit, which runs to the minute. After years of perfect punctuality, the unpredictable timing of the North American transit lines drove me nuts!

Growing Angrier

After several days of dealing with an unreliable schedule, one morning, I verbally tore into my late bus driver, way out of proportion for what was going on that day. I was feeling anger beyond any level of appropriateness, and the bus driver just laughed at my complaints, which made me even angrier.

Out Of Control

I soon realized I was out of control. Showing up for class in an agitated state each morning wasn't the best way to start the next chapter of my life. Remembering my self-sabotaging behaviors in the past, I knew I had to quell my outbursts as I dealt with the challenging reintegration process over the coming weeks and months.

I used the Index to monitor what I *could and couldn't control.* I had the Core Four as my touchstone and realized I needed to make a plan for the bus. So, I allotted extra time for the daily "wait-then-ride" and used it to listen to music or read a book, just like everyone else.

With a better sense of what was within my control and what was reasonable to expect, my frustrations fizzled and my to-and-from became more peaceful.

Sometimes when things feel like they're out of control, it helps to develop a plan that will make you feel *grounded*—or centered. Or just plain *sane.*

Understanding there will be highs and lows (in life, love, and business) makes us realize we're in this for the long-term, not the quick hit. This makes managing all aspects of our lives easier—even the ones we can't control.

Thriving And Growing Vs. Playing It Safe

Once I got my feet under me and got into the rhythm of the Ph.D. program, I couldn't help but think about how my rehab counselor, George, planted the seed years before. I owed a debt of gratitude to the program that helped me open my eyes and reach for a better, more fulfilling life.

Being open to people who know better than me has been a game-changer.

When I get in a tight spot, I often hear the echo: Don't mistake the edge of the rut you're in for the horizon.

So true.

Luckily, I would soon learn there was more to life beyond what I could see directly in front of me.

Now's The Time

When I decided to pursue my doctorate, it was humbling for me. On the first day of grad school, I learned I was not even close to being the smartest person in the room, and it was a new reality for me. Since middle school, I had consistently ranked in the top 10%, but in this class, one woman had earned her Ph.D. in nuclear physics and another had already published his research!

Giving Myself A Break

If I couldn't be the brightest, I *could* work the hardest. Four years later, I was the first to finish school, publish my thesis, and get a job, *thanks to the discipline of using the Index!* I made a plan, took my timetable seriously, and had a mentor who helped me stay focused.

Looking back, keeping the Index and my journal was the key to my success. I loved checking off those goals while reaching for the next one.

In 1999, eight years into recovery, I received my Ph.D. from the University of British Columbia at the age of 35. In 2013, at age 49, I moved to Ann Arbor as a professor of entrepreneurial studies at the top public university in the country.

My reality had exceeded my dreams!

The Personal Sanity Index
Does A Part Of Your Life Feel Like It's Out Of Control?

Reflections on Chapter 15
To get the most out of your PSI, copy this question page and document your reactions to this chapter's content. Take time to consider the questions, answer honestly, and create a journal using these pages as your writing prompts and inspiration.

1. Can you use your Index to give yourself a break? If so, how?

____

____

____

____

____

____

____

____

____

____

____

____

____

Chapter 16

One Minute A Day Will Keep You On Track

One of the positives I hear from people who use the Index, but have suffered from obsessive/addictive compulsions, is how they can be more present in their day-to-day lives because the tracker has their back. They realize it's about developing habits and making them stick, *without having to reserve all of their daily mental focus on achieving their goals.*

In other words, if they have a bad day maintaining their Core Four or PPCs, they realize they can make the next one better and cut themselves some slack. (Consequently, it's also an excellent tool for being kinder to oneself.)

This simple habit prepares you for a motivated, focused, and productive day. It primes your mind for success, making your outcomes more consistent.

One Minute Makes Such A Difference!

It only takes a minute each day to size up your last 24 hours and track them. Some have commented on their ability to improve their health or wealth using the Index and others have found a permanent solution to a decades-old problem.

Before they used the Index, I heard the words "stuck," "anxious," and "failure" a lot. After using it for several months (or even weeks), I hear how they love the simplicity of the PSI in combination with a newfound sense of accomplishment, while feeling more positive about themselves.

When you repeat this review process every day, you will become more focused and your results will become more consistent.

Keeping your workbook in front of you, daily repetition, and measuring the correct input and output are the keys to success.

If you're serious about your quest for a brighter future, keeping track of where you are each day is essential to getting where you want to be.

The Personal Sanity Index
One Minute A Day Will Keep You On Track

Reflections on Chapter 16

To get the most out of your PSI, copy this question page and document your reactions to this chapter's content. Take time to consider the questions, answer honestly, and create a journal using these pages as your writing prompts and inspiration.

1. Are you using your Index consistently every day? Have you discovered anything about your habits or belief system? Explain.

\
\
\
\
\

2. Where have you placed your Index? Is it the best location for you to quickly find it every day?

\
\
\
\
\

Chapter 17

It's All About Taking Action

Remember, change only comes from taking action. The difference between an entrepreneur and everyone else who *thinks* about starting their own business is that the business owner *takes action.*

If the things that make for a great version of you aren't happening, reach out to someone to help you work through it. Often, an extra set of eyes will ensure you don't go off the path. If you feel like a friend or family member won't be understanding about your goal or dream, consider joining a group of like-minded individuals, talk to your spiritual practitioner, or find a mentor. There are even telehealth options if you'd like to seek counseling.

If you're feeling stuck, you will find that a slight change in behavior—starting with your daily habits—will *move mountains* over time.

For example, I find I'm doing things I didn't think were possible for me. My latest goal? I've recently received my commercial helicopter pilot's license. Something that started as an idea (learning to fly) turned into reality (becoming a private pilot) and has grown into something that I hadn't even imagined a few years ago (flying professionally).

As adults, we can have a hard time learning new things and often think we can't make it. As a student pilot, I often felt frustrated and stuck, not knowing if I could master this new skill. When we try new things later in life, we need to *learn how to learn again.*

It's like a muscle that needs exercise.

Every pilot is familiar with checklists similar to the Index. We track all the fluid levels and warning lights *before* starting the engine. The odds of not reaching your destination safely are worse if you don't get all the core things achieved. (Making sure we have enough gas is an essential part of the prep work!) Checklists work because they relieve the burden from our faulty human memories. They work because they include the most important things. But they only work if we use them!

Being A Teacher

I like being a teacher because I'm continually learning, and I'll be happy being a student of life for the rest of my days. I traded my unhealthy addictions for passions, like exercise, and I became a professor to fulfill my constant hunger for knowledge.

But, I also know when *not* to overdo it and I take care of myself. In fact, I've often confessed to my students over the years that, when I was their age and I was considering career choices, I wanted to find a job where I could take naps during the day.

That always gets a laugh in the classroom. But it's funny because it's true. I've discovered that being able to find a few minutes during the day to rest and recover—however you choose to do it—is an indication that you are paying attention to the Core Four and aren't overloading your day.

It's a perfect example of a PPC: *Did I find 20 minutes today to relax my brain?* If you have a hard time answering "Yes" to that question, it might be worth investing some time to understand why, then adding that category to your Index if necessary.

Making Strides

Even though I consider myself a work in progress, when I look back at the strides I've made—thanks to the Index and three simple questions—I can't believe how I've been able to change the trajectory of my life. By taking stock on a regular basis and asking myself **what isn't working for me, what would I rather have, and what I need to do each day to succeed,** I've learned how to stay sober, earn my MBA and Ph.D., become a professor, compete in triathlons, and fly a helicopter.

Dang!

I love being a professor and won't give up my day job anytime soon, but I also love the freedom of reaching for the clouds. It's an excellent metaphor for wanting to have a rocking life and soar like an eagle.

I hope the Index helps you realize your dreams. I'm glad to be part of your quest in discovering the best version of you while helping you maintain your personal sanity.

# # #

The Personal Sanity Index
It's All About Taking Action

Reflections on Chapter 17

To get the most out of your PSI, copy this question page and document your reactions to this chapter's content. Take time to consider the questions, answer honestly, and create a journal using these pages as your writing prompts and inspiration.

1. If you're unable to make the changes you desire, is there someone you can reach out to for help?

____

____

____

2. Feel free to update your Index as necessary. What are the three critical questions you can ask yourself at least twice a year as the foundation of your continual quest for personal improvement?

____

____

____

____

____

Addendum

Why Is *Expecting* Variation The Key
To Achieving Success (And Staying Sane)?

When reaching or achieving our long-desired goals, unexpected downward trends can serve as the perfect excuse to throw caution to the wind and return to old behaviors. But most people don't realize that variations are *normal* and should be expected instead of being considered a point of "failure," leading to the much-dreaded backslide and undoing all previous success.

How PSI Works

The principles underlying the Personal Sanity Index are drawn from the laws of statistics and their Quality Assurance applications in manufacturing. As an engineer, I used the tools of statistical process control for years. The reason most of the world's leading companies use these techniques is because they work, they are reliable, and they're simple to use.

So, how does it work?

First, you need a process or activity that is regular and repeatable, e.g., a machine that makes the same part over and over or your daily commute to work. For each of these examples, there's an average measurement one could take: *inches* for the machine part or *time* for the commute. If you take daily measurements and plot them on a chart, you'd likely see something like the illustration in **Figure 3—Daily Commuting Time** (page 104). I've used the example of commuting since it's something most of us have experienced.

We can experience temporary disruptions in many aspects of our lives. When looking at Figure 3, there are a few things we can observe right away. First, no two measurements (in this case, commuting time) are exactly the same. Some days it takes a little more time; other days, a little less. That's normal, *natural* variation, just as the daily temperature varies in a given season.

The other main feature of this type of graph is that there is an average, or typical, amount of time for the commute. Using our temperature example, in July, the daily averages are warmer than in January, and the monthly average is similar from one year to the next.

Changes In Average

It may seem simple and obvious, but those two features—average and daily *variance*—are common to most things in our lives. And that's what we'll see if we build an effective PSI.

In your PSI, include factors that you often accomplish but may not achieve every day. If you include items in your Index that you never achieve (or always do), you won't have any variance, and *tracking variance is the key!* For example, if you think meditation is a good idea, but you've never done it and you don't even know how to start, that might not be a great item to include. But if meditation is something you often do, but not always, it could be a great candidate.

That's the thinking behind the Core Four. We know that we are healthier when we sleep well, eat well, exercise, and connect with others. But we don't always hit our goals with each of them, or all of them, every day. If we try to improve our consistency with these behaviors, our average score should increase—*but there will still be daily variation.*

That's one important way charts can help us—we can see changes in average.

Stay Sane By Expecting Variance

I live in a college town, so there aren't many people around in the summer. The first two weeks in the chart were recorded in late August and the average travel time was about 25 minutes. But look what happens when we get to the end of summer and students return for fall classes. More people means more cars on the road, which leads to longer commuting times. There's still variation from day to day, depending on whether I hit red or green lights, if there are more or fewer people using crosswalks, whether it's raining or not, etc. But it consistently takes longer in September than it does in August. An external influence causes that: in this case, students returning to campus.

PSI: Lows And Highs

Sometimes, shifts in average can indicate a permanent or long-term change. Other times, there may be a temporary cause for the shift. Figure 3 also shows a week when the average commute time increased by several minutes and then returned to the previous level. The cause, in this case, was road construction.

The PSI shows us how certain factors influence our overall state of health and well-being. The first year I lived in Ann Arbor, I rented a house that was close to a railway crossing. Sometimes, late at night, a train would roll through, sounding its horn and jolting me awake. That negatively affected my sleep and kept my PSI average score low.

Since then, I've moved to a quieter part of town, well away from the tracks, and my sleep improved dramatically. Some nights, I still don't get great sleep—so there's still variance—but the average is definitely better!

Pay Attention To The Signals

There are two additional signals we can pick up on from a well-designed chart. The first is "trends," and the other is "change in variance." Trends can alert us to changes as they are starting to happen.

In the commuting example in Figure 3, you can see the trend to longer travel times began during the last week of August. As more students returned, traffic volume increased and it took a little longer each day to get to work. Eventually, the trend leveled off at the new normal and regular variation returned. Trends are typically indicated by three or more consecutive observations in the same direction, increasing or decreasing. The road construction didn't signal the shift with a leading trend—it just happened. But it also went away just as suddenly. Trends aren't always there to warn us that a change is coming, but if we see a pattern in our PSI where the daily scores are steadily changing, it might be worth taking time to figure out why.

How This Translates

Increasing workloads can sneak up on us. We do a little more each day to stay on top of things or catch up when we fall behind. Maybe that means skipping a workout, or grabbing some fast food on the way home from work, or staying up later than usual. These factors will add up, and the change will be obvious if we are paying attention to the PSI chart. We can't always take action to change the demands of work, but sometimes we can. And, at the very least, being aware that we're not looking after ourselves as well as we should can help us make the extra effort to squeeze in a workout, eat a healthy meal, or get to bed a little earlier.

Changes In Variance

So far, we've been looking at changes in average. Those changes can be short or long-term, sudden or gradual. The charts can help us see them when they happen, though it's up to us to figure out the cause. Sometimes it's obvious (e.g., road construction); in other cases, we never quite understand what has caused a change to occur.

Change in variance is something else altogether. In many ways, it's harder to spot, and the consequences of increased variance can be severe. Returning one final time to the commuting example, you can see in Figure 3 that the *range* of daily times is more extensive after the road construction than it was earlier that month. It has become less *predictable*, and that increases the chances of arriving late to work. It's harder to plan for big swings than to work within a standard set of expected outcomes.

Using the PSI, if I am in a regular rhythm of routine with an **average score of 4** (that moves up or down by one or two points each day), that's a pretty good place for me to be. But if my daily ups and downs (variance) increase to **plus or minus three points with no predictability,** that is the definition of out-of-control, especially if I don't know what's causing it. Increased variance usually has a cause, just like changes in average have a cause. And sometimes the reasons are obvious. For a machine tool, it could be as simple as a loose guide. Once the problem is discovered, the errant part can be fixed and the process brought back under control.

I've had times when increased PSI variance can be traced to an obvious cause. For example, hosting family members in my home for an extended period can throw a wrench into daily routines, but at least that's easy to understand and has an end in sight. *But when there's no apparent reason for the change,* that is perhaps the most critical time to invest in self-discovery to track down the cause(s) and bring things back under control. Friends and family can be great resources at times like this. Things that are invisible to us can be *obvious* to the people around us.

Tracking Behaviors To Make Better Choices

Figure 4 (page 105) captures all of the elements we've been discussing in my Personal Sanity Index. I've pulled these actual examples together from different times in my life (remember, I've been doing this for decades). If I can see a trend or a shift, at least I have a chance to do something about it. For me, that's the real value—and magic—of the PSI.

In my journey, I've seen disruptions caused by work travel that affect sleep, exercise, nutrition, and my connection to others. It's easy to spot during the second week in Figure 4. On Monday of that week, I only managed a score of 2—below the range I'd like it to be.

In this case, sleep was disrupted by being in an unfamiliar hotel room, food was a combination of a greasy breakfast buffet and heavy restaurant meals for lunch and dinner. Also, I didn't find time to connect with family or friends, much less get to the gym. I was so out of sorts from all those disruptions that I really wasn't feeling very grateful.

The only two areas where I gave myself points for the day were learning and quiet time. Hotels may not be great for a first night's sleep, but they do provide an oasis of solitude. And it's hard to engage well in a work project without learning new things, so that was also a positive aspect of the day. So, Monday was a score of two (quiet and learning) and the rest of the week followed a similar pattern. Another period of disruption can be observed in week four, when my house was full of loving but demanding family members.

On the other hand, vacation often provides an opportunity to invest time in self-care (week five), and my daily Index scores are frequently highest when I'm away from the demands of work. My score was a very healthy 6 on Monday of vacation week. I was able to invest time in almost all aspects of my Index that day. The only exception was eating, because I went back for extra helpings at the breakfast buffet.

In summary, our well-being is reflected in and influenced by our daily behaviors. Keeping an eye on patterns, especially trends and changes in averages, can help us maintain a healthier, happier, and more balanced state. It's been helping me through 30 years of ups and downs, and I hope it can also be of some benefit to you, especially if it helps you maintain your personal sanity.

For more information, go to personalsanityindex.com.

Figure 3

Daily Commuting Time
Summertime. Average commute = 25 minutes.
Students begin to return. Commuting time increases.
New avg. commute = 32 min.
Road repairs.
Increased variance in travel time.
45:00
40:00
35:00
30:00
25:00
20:00
15:00

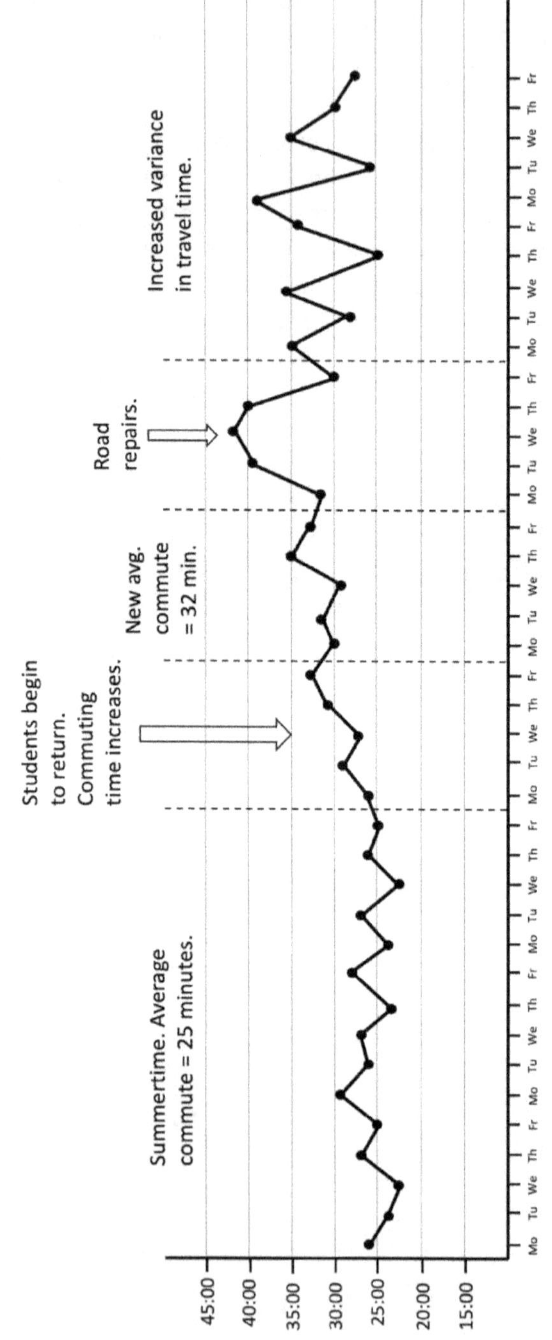

Figure 4

Stewart's Personal Sanity Index
Business
travel
Hosting
house guests
Vacation

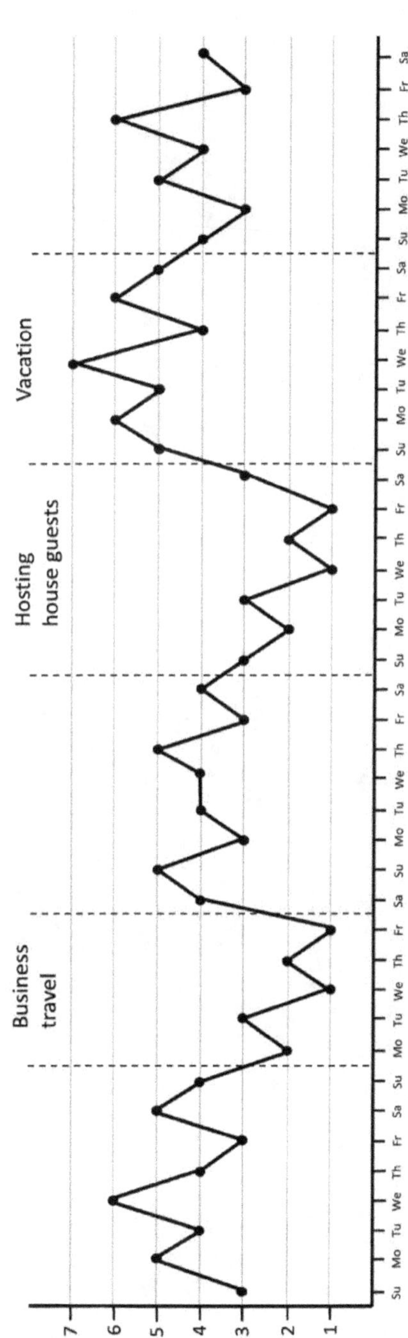

Endnotes

[1] *US Centers for Disease Control and Prevention (CDC); "Obesity is a common, serious, and costly disease"; https://www.cdc.gov/obesity/data/adult.html*

[2] *National Center for Biotechnology Information, U.S. National Library of Medicine; Adam Biener, Ph.D., John Cawley, Ph.D., Chad Meyerhoefer, Ph.D.; "The High and Rising Costs of Obesity to the US Health Care System"; https://www.ncbi.nlm.nih.gov/pmc/articles/PMC5359159/*

[3] *US Centers for Disease Control and Prevention (CDC); "Exercise or Physical Activity"; https://www.cdc.gov/nchs/fastats/exercise.htm*

[4] *National Center for Biotechnology Information, U.S. National Library of Medicine; Rand Health Quarterly; Marco Hafner, Martin Stepanek, Jirka Taylor, Wendy M. Troxel, Christian van Stolk; "Why Sleep Matters—The Economic Costs of Insufficient Sleep: A Cross-Country Comparative Analysis"; https://www.ncbi.nlm.nih.gov/pmc/articles/PMC5627640/*

[5] *National Center for Biotechnology Information, U.S. National Library of Medicine; EMBO Reports; Sebastian Trautmann, Jürgen Rehm, Hans-Ulrich Wittchen; "The economic costs of mental disorders: Do our societies react appropriately to the burden of mental disorders?"; https://www.ncbi.nlm.nih.gov/pmc/articles/PMC5007565/*

[6] *US Centers for Disease Control and Prevention (CDC); Sleep and Sleep Disorders, Data and Statistics; https://www.cdc.gov/sleep/data_statistics.html*

[7] *CDC; "Strategies to Prevent Obesity and Other Chronic Diseases: The CDC Guide to Strategies to Increase the Consumption of Fruits and Vegetables"; Atlanta: U.S. Department of Health and Human Services; https://www.cdc.gov/obesity/downloads/strategies-fruits-and-vegetables.pdf*

[8] *CDC; Physical Activity; "How Much Physical Activity Do Adults Need?"; https://www.cdc.gov/physicalactivity/basics/adults/index.htm*

[9] *The Center For Compassion And Altruism Research And Education, Stanford Medicine; Dr. Emma Seppala, "Connectedness & Health: The Science of Social Connection"; http://ccare.stanford.edu/uncategorized/connectedness-health-the-science-of-social-connection-infographic/*

[10] *Psychology Today; Yana Hoffman, RP, C.C.D.C, Hank Davis, Ph.D., "Emotional Connections Make Us Healthier"; https://www.psychologytoday.com/us/blog/try-see-it-my-way/201911/emotional-connections-make-us-healthier*

About The Author
Stewart Thornhill, Ph.D.

Stewart Thornhill, Ph.D., is the Eugene Applebaum Professor of Entrepreneurial Studies at the University of Michigan. *The Personal Sanity Index* (PSI) is based on decades of research and personal experience, drawing on Dr. Thornhill's journey from manufacturing engineer to business school professor and entrepreneur.

The Personal Sanity Index is a daily accountability system that helps the user reach or maintain success with the added benefit of alerting them to the possibility of veering off course *before it happens.* Based on the principles of Quality Assurance after having used it for years as an engineer, Thornhill was aware of the powerful capabilities of the program and used it to create the best version of himself, going after far-reaching goals and what seemed like insurmountable challenges.

As a result, he's developed a 30-year continuous improvement program with a personalized approach to well-being that has helped him flourish and thrive in the face of significant obstacles and life challenges. Over time he has been able to maintain his sobriety, earn his MBA and Ph.D., compete in triathlons, and become a professor and a helicopter pilot.

For more information, visit personalsanityindex.com.